CIVIL
LINES
5

CIVIL LINES

New Writing from India

5

Edited by
Kai Friese and Mukul Kesavan

IndiaInk

CIVIL LINES 5
Edited by Kai Friese & Mukul Kesavan

ISBN 81-86939-10-5

© CIVIL LINES, 2001

CIVIL LINES
New Writing from India
a series

Editorial Collective
Dharma Kumar
Ivan Hutnik
Kai Friese
Mukul Kesavan
Rukun Advani
D-28, Oxford Apartments, 11, I.P. Extension, Delhi 110092

Published for the editors, CIVIL LINES
by IndiaInk,
an imprint of RST IndiaInk Publishing Co. Pvt. Ltd.
B-57 New Rajinder Nagar, New Delhi 110060

Designed by Itu Chaudhuri Design
Printed and bound by Thomson Press (India) Ltd.

Contents

CONTENTS

For their general enthusiasm and financial support to *Civil Lines*
we'd like to thank

THE HINDU
(specifically Nirmala Lakshman)

and

THE BRITISH COUNCIL
(specifically Edmund Marsden, Nic Humphries and Rajni Badlani)

Other potential patrons of the literate needy who happen to read this
page should contact us at once, before they find the next issue is out.

Picador acquires publication rights to the frontlist and backlist of one of the most important living writers in the *English Language:* V.S. Naipaul's, his new novel, *Half a Life,* to be published in hardback in September 2001. Picador will also be the publishers of V.S. Naipaul's backlist; an extraordinary body of work of more than fifteen titles including *A House for Mr. Biswas, A Bend in the River, The Middle Passage and An Area of Darkness.* The backlist will be republished by Picador over the next three years.

Orders to:
India Book Distributors
(Bombay) Limited
1007/1008 Arcadia
195 Nariman Point
Mumbai - 400 121
Tel: 022-282 4646/4691/5220
Fax: 022-287 2531
e-mail: ibd@vsnl.com

Enquiries to:
Rajdeep Mukherjee
Pan Macmillan
5A/12 Ansari Road
Daryaganj
New Delhi - 110 002
Tel: 011-325 9643
Telefax: 011-327 2010
e-mail: panmacmillan@vsnl.com

PICADOR INDIA

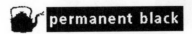 permanent black

Beyond Nationalist Frames: Postmodernism, Hindutva, History
(forthcoming)

ASHIS NANDY
Time Warps: The Politics of Silent and Evasive Pasts
(forthcoming)

AMITAV GHOSH
The Imam and the Indian and Other Essays
(forthcoming)

MADHAV GADGIL
*Environmental Journeys: The Science and Politics of
Conservation in India*

TANIKA SARKAR
*Hindu Wife, Hindu Nation: Community, Religion and
Cultural Nationalism*

RAMACHANDRA GUHA
An Anthropologist Among the Marxists and Other Essays

MAHESH RANGARAJAN
India's Wildlife History: An Introduction

FRANCIS ROBINSON
The Ulama of Farangi Mahall and Islamic Culture in South Asia

SHARAT CHANDRA CHATTERJEE
The Final Question ('Shesh Prashna'), translated from Bengali
by Sukanta Chaudhuri *et al.*

MAULVI NAZIR AHMED
The Bride's Mirror ('Mirat ul-Arus': the first Urdu bestseller),
with an Afterword by Frances W. Pritchett
(forthcoming)

FRENCH
INF•RMAT ON
RESOURCE
CENTRE

FRENCH INFORMATION RESOURCE CENTRE

French Information Resource Centre (FIRC) is a fully equipped lending library and resource centre that favours free exchange of people's ideas and cultures. Its main aim is to provide valuable and up-to-date information about France to all those who need it, both for leisure and professional purposes.

Therefore, the focus is mainly on the most contemporary aspects of France with an increasing part of the collection in English language. In addition to the 8 000 books and a hundred titles of periodicals, a vast music collection is offered, which includes French classical music, jazz, rock, rap and folk. So is a sizeable stock of fiction and documentary films, most of which are subtitled in English.

FIRC also offers efficient computerised public access catalogue, Internet access facility and more than 300 CD-ROMs for consultation.

Its information service answers, free of cost, any queries, related to contemporay France simply by writing or sending fax/e-mail. As a part of a wider information network, it also benefits the assistance of the Bibliothèque Publique d'Information in Paris, which can provide the information that is not available in our centres in India.

Since a most important objective of FIRC is to play a meeting point for Indian and French culture, emphasise is given on literature. A vast collection of books covering all the periods of French literature, poetry and fiction is available at the library in French and their English translations as well.

This is complimented with the organisation of "literary cafés" in the library. A particular theme is chosen every month and texts pertaining to the theme are read followed by discussions. The first **"literary café"** with the theme "Libertinism and dandyism" will be held on **14th September** at **6:30 p.m.** at the FIRC.

We also invite both Indian and French literature lovers to participate in a special training **"Lire à voix haute"** from **16th to 20th October 2001** conducted by a professor of the **Sorbonne University, Paris**. The programme will be on reading French literary texts aloud.

Please feel free to contact us for any further information.

Manisha Narayan
French Information Resource Centre
Embassy of France- Cultural Services
2 Aurangzeb Road
New Delhi 110 011
Ph: 301 56 31 / 301 46 82
Fax: 379 38 92
E-mail: france@vsnl.com
Web site: http://www.france-in-india.org

Liberté - Égalité - Fraternité
RÉPUBLIQUE FRANÇAISE

Embassy of France in India

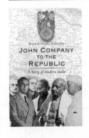

First 🐧 Fiction

The Hottest Day of the Year
Brinda Charry
- Brilliant first novel
- Brinda Charry has won the Katha Award for Creative Fiction

0670 912360
Rs 250

The Web of Silk & Gold

Shakti Nilanjana
- First novel written with insight, honesty and great sensitivity
- a young woman's heart-rending journey from innocence to maturity and strength

0140 293272
Rs 200

The Tutor of History
Manjushree Thapa
- A first novel of great maturity and sophistication marking the arrival of a significant new voice
- The first major novel in English to emerge from Nepal.

0141 007745
Rs 295

The Story of Noble Rot

Uzma Aslam Khan
- vividly narrated and full of funny yet complex dilemmas
- marks the debut of a gifted storyteller from Pakistan

0141 00567X
Rs 200

the best in new writing from the subcontinent

Penguin Books India
11 Community Centre, Panchsheel Park, New Delhi 110017
www.penguinbooksindia.com

Skin

The Evening Gone

The Seduction of Silence

The Opium Clerk

Introduction

CIVIL LINES 5 begins with Sonia Jabbar on life and death in contemporary Kashmir and ends with Urvashi Butalia revisiting partition. In between these two non-fictional narratives are short stories by Mina Kumar, Amit Chaudhuri, Suketu Mehta, Amitava Kumar and Avtar Singh and Anita Roy's reconstruction of her encounters with the American writer, Harold Brodkey. (An early editorial rule at Civil Lines was that it wouldn't publish writing about writing, i.e. criticism. We don't think Anita Roy's obsessive engagement with Brodkey breaks that rule: readerly fixation is fine; it is critical appreciation that terrifies us.) We think that the seven stories in this issue add up to the best and most diverse collection of short fiction you're likely to read till... well, till Civil Lines 6 comes along.

As far as we can tell—we haven't met every one of our contributors—this issue of Civil Lines is gender-balanced: four men, four women. Four stories have American settings which will encourage rooted critics in their belief that Indian fiction in English (spelt IFIE, pronounced 'iffy') is an expatriate art. Even the non-fiction happens elsewhere: Urvashi's piece is set in Pakistan, Anita's in England and America, and the issue opens with Kashmir, the Indian-ness of which is chronically and violently contested.

Civil Lines advertises itself as New Writing from India. This is misleading (as most advertisements are) because in its short life Civil Lines has been host to old writing newly translated, writing by not-Indian writers, writing by Indians Elsewhere and so on. It is a good time to fret publicly about identity because Civil Lines is bidding to become respectable by becoming regular. Instead of happening at eccentric intervals, Civil Lines will appear twice a year—give or take a month or two. Those who read Civil Lines 4 will have noticed that Civil Lines 5 appears in the same calendar year. This might seem unremarkable to some but when you consider that three years passed between Civil Lines 3 & 4, it is measurable progress. There's every reason to believe that the next issue will appear in the summer of 2002. This issue has been made possible by the generosity of the Hindu and the British Council whose grants have helped subsidize our costs.

But to return to the question of content so that anyone who plans to write for Civil Lines (or, for that matter, to read it regularly) will have some sense of what it is likely to publish. Civil Lines will publish good writing by desis (loosely defined to include all kinds of south Asians), it will publish anyone (Indian or otherwise) whose work has something to do with our part of the world and (just to make things really precise) it will publish anything the editors like.

SONIA JABBAR

Spirit of Place

1. The Path

IT IS AUTUMN and I'm hovering somewhere between the 9th and 14th centuries, recovering some of Kashmir's rich past in my explorations of ancient sites and still more ancient people—amateur historians, mythologists, anchorites, all. It is truly fascinating and far more engaging than the dreadful accounting of killings and tortures that has occupied me all year. The weather is gorgeous. Brilliant sunshine and a cold that nips pleasurably. The gigantic chinars and poplars are turning to rust and gold. Great flocks of sheep and long-haired goats swarm down from the high pastures, flooding the plains, drowning the highways so that even now, on this road to Ganderbal, the Maruti and the bus in front are transformed into little islands in this vast woolly sea, lapping and eddying around us. It is a while before the shepherds, the Gujjars, with their great curving noses and hennaed beards, whistle their flock into remarkable discipline.

The wait, though, isn't without some trepidation. Kumarji and I sitting in front, could pass off as anybody—we have nothing that distinguishes our religion. But the ladies crammed into the back seat, the old ladies who have gossiped and giggled and sung bhajans off-key this past hour? Sari clad, tikas, and worse still, the unmistakable mark of the Kashmiri Pandit woman, the dejehor, heavy triangular earrings suspended by a complex system of gold chains. In Srinagar this would have been passable but we are in Ganderbal and Lar is only a stone's throw away. The same Lar which, according to some, could be Kandahar, so infested is it with Afghan Mujahideen, their fingers welded to hair-triggers. But the ladies are sanguine. "Bhagvati kare theek," they shrug, and we are, after all going to visit Bhagvati, Devi, Ragni, Khir Bhavani, the great benign mother in her shrine at Tula Mula. It is this spirit of optimism and resilience that has kept the handful of Kashmiri Pandits—17,860 to be precise—in the Valley. I am tending to spend more and more time with them these days, watching them negotiate and nourish the old relationships with the Muslims, worn thin by the decade of war, dirty politics and mistrust. Watching also, their anger and disbelief at being scorned and targeted by the Pandits who fled the Valley in the early 1990s to the refugee camps of Jammu and Delhi.

It was at a refugee settlement in Jammu that I first realised the importance of Khir Bhavani for the Kashmiri Pandits. My host was Shekhar, a soft-spoken, bespectacled, middle-aged man. I'd thought of spending an hour or so with him but ended up five hours later unable to tear myself away from the unending stream of stories, anecdotes, myths, histories. How different he seemed now from his earlier avatar that I had encountered in various fora on Kashmir: the strident Dr. Agnishekhar, convener of Panun Kashmir, demagogue, agitator for a separate Pandit homeland. We had kept our respective politics intact and yet laughed quietly together this afternoon. Now we were parting as friends. "Wait. Don't go yet. I want to show you something." He slipped into his chappals and walked out of the front door into the warm evening, "I know you'll enjoy this." We walked up the narrow street, negotiating piles of building material. The colony was desolate, a treeless wasteland. On either side were the newly built, single-storeyed, pill-box homes of the refugees, abject substitutes for the ancient, soaring, four-tiered houses of Anantnag, or Safa Kadal, Bijbehara or Sattu Barbarshah: delicate brick-worked, latticed-windowed, wooden-tile-roofed structures gravitating lovingly towards each other.

"What's this?" I said as we stood under a small rise on top of which I could see the marble trikoned canopy of a temple. We trotted up the steps, Shekhar greeting the evening temple-goers. At last we stood at the gate and with a great theatrical swoop of the arm, he said, "Welcome to Khir Bhavani, Jammu." I entered, speechless, and stood silently watching a few men and women at prayer; the gaudy fairy lights illuminating their faces deeply absorbed in devotion. In front of me stood an exact replica of Khir Bhavani—smaller than the original, but faithful in detail. The holy spring out of which the original temple grew was replaced here by a tank filled with tap water. All form and no content. A wave of sadness washed over me. It was suddenly perfectly clear. This wasn't any old temple. They missed Kashmir so badly that they had tried to replicate it here, like children with their dolls' houses, entering a world at once real and make-believe. It was like the old Pandit woman in a camp in Delhi who confessed that she could only make it through the hideous summers by sitting in front of the cooler, closing her eyes tightly and imagining that it was cool Kashmiri rain and not the wet machine-propelled air caressing her face. The rage follows quickly after disappointment when the eyes fly open and it is not Kashmir at all but a stinking cooler in a stinking room in a stinking refugee camp far, far away from Kashmir. At some point each one must have realised that it is not a question of a few weeks or months but perhaps forever that the gates of Kashmir have been slammed shut behind them. Now that I have lived in Kashmir I understand their irreparable sense of loss and longing, of betrayal and heartbreak. I understand now the anger of the refugee, their bitterness towards all who were fortunate enough to remain in the Valley, be they Muslims or Hindus. I don't know what is worse: to lose a beloved, to lose a father or a son, or to lose one's entire universe.

2. The Circumambulation

Ravan had the audacity to try and bribe the Goddess to work the forces of the universe on his side as Ram battered down the gates of Lanka with his army of monkeys. The Goddess, appalled by Ravan's evil deeds was in no mood to be propitiated and flew into a rage. Ravan tried his best to appease her, but She would have none of it, or of him, or of Lanka, and ordered Hanuman to fly her out of the wretched isle as far away as possible. They flew far north into the Himalayas—Hanuman, the Goddess and her 360 serpents—

and alighted, it seems, in the most felicitous of places, Tula Mula, where the Goddess has remained since.

But it wasn't until a pious brahman, Krishna Pandit—in some unspecified period of antiquity—had a visitation by the Devas, that the site became known to humans.

"How shall I find the spring?" he had asked the Gods, trembling with excitement.

"Engage a boat as far as Shadipor, and from there a serpent will guide you. Thus shall you know."

He did as he was told, engaged a boat and came as far as Shadipor, and behold! a snake was seen to be swimming in the waters of the swamp. The boat followed the snake. The snake halt-ed at particular places where Krishna Pandit fixed long sticks into the swamp to demarcate the area. Thus was the divine spring dis-covered. Then the intrepid Pandit set about reclaiming the land by dumping dry earth into the marsh. When the ground was pre-pared, he brought wide-eyed devotees from Srinagar to worship the Goddess. As soon as the puja ended Krishna Pandit opened his eyes and found a piece of birch bark floating on the waters of the spring. On retrieving it he found a sloka written on it, describ-ing the divine form of the goddess Ragni.

> I make obeisance to that one Goddess who,
> having taken the position of the Supreme God
> is the Queen in reality, whose form is made of light and is
> adorned by (the lustre of) twelve suns,
> who cannot be observed through senses,
> who is seated on a throne and is wrapped with serpents[1].

It is said that the spring was once surrounded by 360 springs. Now it is surrounded by the bunkers of the Border Security Force. Gaily painted signs welcome us as we approach a sand-bagged booth to sign ourselves in. Name, State, M/F, Time In, Time Out, Sign. It feels like the register at the heavily guarded gates of the secretariat in Srinagar. But nothing can spoil our mood, and I follow the excited chattering old ladies into an enclosed area at the edge of the temple wall that says "For women only". In no time they have stripped down to their underwear, great breasts flapping against wobbling stomachs as they plunge into the icy waters of the canal to purify themselves. I realise—with some alarm—that I am expected to follow suit. It is far too cold and I decide to put up with their withering glances instead. I bring the women fists full of earth that serves as soap, and also help one of the toothless ladies out of the contraptions that hold her broken old body together: neck collar, spine brace, left knee brace, right knee brace, elastic crêpe bandage around the left ankle. She chuckles loudly at my obvious discomfiture before pinching the tip of her nose, taking a voluminous gulp of air and disappearing under the dark waters of the Gangkhai.

✤

I first heard about Hamid the Fish after he had been shot dead by the security forces. They claimed that it was he who had master-minded the killing of 23 Pandits in Wandhama in January of '98. It was spring and I think the event was sandwiched between reports of Fidayeen attacks and the dreadful massacre of Chittisinghpora. It would have escaped my notice except that the local newspapers had made much of the fact of him ducking the security dragnet for eleven years. There were just a handful of the old guard left among the militants. Most had been killed by the army and para-military or by rival Mujahideen groups just a few years into the insurgency. The cleverer ones surrendered, joined the pro-state Ikhwan, only to be picked off one by one by determined assassins over the years. The cleverest were like Hamid the Fish, or Yusuf Chopan of Bandipora, Robin Hood-like characters, determined, incorruptible, striking terror into the hearts of their enemies but never, it is said, harassing innocents, silently cheered on by the vil-lagers of the area they controlled. A forest of legends grew up swiftly around them, so that it was impossible to hear a story about one or the other without the appellation of ferishta, or angel, added to their names. This is rare in Kashmir: one usually hears the army and the militants being cursed in the same breath.

"Even in death Yusuf Chopan was compassionate and heroic," Haleema had said softly, "The army had cordoned off the house. He knew that they would have used mortars and blown us all up if he'd remained holed up inside. So he made a dash for it with the other guy. They leapt out of this window. The snow was deep and the dawn light made them easy targets, dark silhouettes against the whiteness..."

She pointed to the field behind the house, "This where they fell. There was fresh snow, white, pure white. But they pumped so many bullets into him to make sure he was dead, that the field turned red."

"So, when did they take your husband away?"

"Right after. They accused us of being accomplices but what could we do? Yusuf came at 3 in the morning and demanded food.

They have guns too. I woke up and fed him and allowed him to rest for a bit, that's all. What could we do?"

This is Buthu, Bandipora District in North Kashmir, a couple of hours hard climb through the forest from Aham Sharif. Because there is no road, the village remains isolated and at the mercy of both the militants and security forces who swoop down with tiresome frequency. Shaafi and I sat eating hot rotis and a delicious local saag. We were famished after the walk. It was a warm summer night and I was propped drowsily against the window half-listening to the delightfully secular young Maulvi's monologue and drifting into a delicious feeling of well-being. A fat, buttery moon painted the pine-covered hillsides in dramatic shades of silver and shadow. Suddenly, I thought I heard something which made me sit bolt upright, straining to hear above the conversation, the clinks from the kitchen and the insistent chirping of crickets. A half minute went by before I heard it again. A ghostly wail which echoed in the hills and made my hair stand on end.

"What's that?" I said.

The men looked up quizzically, unwilling to break the talk.

"Listen." I said with a growing sense of unease.

Nothing. After a few minutes of politely humouring me they return to the gossiping. I begin to feel a bit foolish when I hear it again. And again.

"Listen! What was that?"

"Probably jackals."

The man at the hookah giggles nervously.

"Ha didi, it's probably chudails or ghosts!" Shaafi teases.

But then they hear it. The Maulvi jumps up and walks swiftly outside. He stands on the step frowning but perfectly still. The

10

wail echoes again and the Maulvi explodes into life, rushing inside and shuttering the windows. Like a well-rehearsed drill all the actors, without a word spoken, leap up and dash about.

"What... what's going on...Shaafi, what is it dammit? Someone say something."

Everyone is tight-lipped. I hear the banging of doors and windows, creaking of bolts sliding shut, thumping of seven or eight pairs of little feet on wooden stairs as the children run to hide in the attic. Then, silence and stillness but for the women weeping and whimpering in each others' arms in the corners. The lamps are turned out. We sit quietly in the darkness, neck-deep in fear. I can feel my heart slow down, my breath shallow, my senses expanded.

"It sounds like something's happening in the mohalla above us," the Maulvi whispers.

"What?"

"I don't know. Maybe an RR raid."

"At this hour?"

"Always at this hour."

We wait. The minutes drag on. We hear the shrieking again, clearer this time, inhuman cries. I can't bear it any longer and get up.

"Where d' you think you're going?" the Maulvi hisses.

"I have to find out. I must see..."

"Sit down," he pulls me roughly by the wrist. "Don't be foolish. We'll find out in the morning."

A couple of hours later, a group of wailing women and men come down the path in front of the house. It seems it is safe now to step out. The Maulvi is soon surrounded by them and speaks in low comforting tones. They hold mashaals, burning torches, in their hands, the flickering light throwing ghostly shadows on their tear-stained faces. The story unfolds jerkily, but in the end I gather that the paramilitary Rashtriya Rifles had done a cordon-and-search operation. A couple of rough Ikhwanis went in first looking for Manzoor Ahmed Reshi while the RR stood guard outside. He was asleep. They woke him up, told him to dress at gunpoint while the women wailed and pleaded with them not to take him away.

"Don't worry. The sahab just wants to ask him a few questions outside. He'll be back after five or ten minutes," one of the men said soothingly. Then the whole lot disappeared swiftly into the night. That's when the wails and screams started. The village had had some experience of this. The Maulvi's brother had been taken one night a couple of years ago in exactly the same manner. They found him the next morning, face down, barely a hundred yards from the village with a bullet through his head.

Poor Manzoor Ahmed Reshi, the carpenter who can no longer ply his trade. The man whose arm hangs limply at his side because it was shot up in the cross-fire five years ago by God alone knows whose bullets. The same man who was picked up a year ago and shown a photograph.

"Know this face?"

"Yes."

"Is he with you?"

"No."

"Does he come often?"

"Yes."

"Go now and when Chopan comes into the village next I want

you to inform us."

When Chopan was killed, retribution followed swiftly. They picked up Reshi one night and beat him mercilessly. He pleaded with the militants to let him go, that he was innocent and had nothing to do with Chopan's betrayal. Perhaps they believed him because he returned, bleeding and battered, but alive.

Sitting in the dusty courtyard the morning following the nightmare I had witnessed, I promised Reshi's young wife that I'd follow up on the case, and that she shouldn't lose heart, that I was sure he'd return just fine: words I have repeated so often these last five years. Earnestly. Then I went up the hill to see Haleema.

The house was double-storeyed, as Kashmiri peasant houses tend to be, with a large courtyard full of clucking chickens. The woman looked worn out and frail as she recounted the tale of Chopan's last stand and the subsequent arrest of her husband. The room was neat and gaily painted. On one wall, in red paint, in English, neatly printed, with laurels in green on either side, was written: *You only live once, but if you live right once is enough.*

"Who wrote this?" I asked, struck by the terrible irony.

"I did," Haleema's sixteen year old son, Hilal, said shyly.

"Your English is very good, as is your writing, but your wisdom is even better."

He smiled, "Actually, my father used to say that."

I turned to Haleema just before I left, "By the way, what charge did they take your husband on?"

She excused herself for a few minutes and rummaging in an old trunk pulled out a copy of the FIR. It had been lodged by the Naib Subedar, S.S. Rawat of the 14 Rashtriya Rifles camped at Chittarnar, under the Indian Arms Act 7/25 and Act 307—212 RPC.

ABBAR

It recommended nine months for Wali under the Public Safety
Act. Naib Subedar Rawat accused Wali Mohammed Reshi of sedi-
tion: "Mohd. Wali Reshi incites militants against India."

✛

3. The Gates

This is marvellous. My neck starts to hurt because I've been looking up in wonder for the last five minutes. The chinars were plant-
ed with some design in mind because now, several hundred years
later, together they form a grand marquee. The sky shows only in
tiny irregular fragments of blue. The light filtering in is a cool
green. The flagstones are so cold that they hurt my naked feet.
Behind me is the Gangkhai arcing around the periphery of the
temple, forming a natural moat. I turn to look at the ducks quack-
ing and fussing among the reeds when a voice says: "The canal
protects the temple. Whenever it has been attacked, the bullets
and shells have landed harmlessly in these waters."

I turn to see the man who has been selling Kumarji flowers and
incense grinning at me.

"Really, it's true," he says emphatically. "This place is very special."

I grin back and buy a plateful of flowers. The old ladies are
making a huge racket ringing the temple bells vigorously. I follow
behind them, touching the temple bell above me to announce my
presence to the Goddess gingerly. I don't really believe but I've
always been a sucker for ritual.

The temple is actually no temple. A wide courtyard with flagstones and the chinars surrounds the spring which is no more than

14

twenty-five feet long and fifteen wide. The spring is an irregular septagon with its apex at the east curiously called pad, or feet. At its opposite end is the sher or head. The northern and southern sides are longer. On an island in the centre is a tiny shrine to the Goddess. Once a mulberry tree grew here ("Tul = Mulberry, and Mul = Roots," Kumarji told me.) Yellow and orange marigolds overflow from it, tumbling into the spring. The Goddess peeks out from among them: a small delicate figurine in bronze, said to have been recovered from the waters. Facing the shrine at the edge of the spring is a narrow pavilion in which we stand now, hands folded, heads bowed. The Purohit is chanting raucously in Sanskrit. Kumarji and I exchange glances. "The Mahant is on leave today so we'll have to make do with the BSF Purohit," he whispers. I steal a glance at the old ladies. They are blissed out: eyes closed, beatific smiles, swaying to the grating voice of the Purohit. From time to time he instructs us to light the diyas, drop flowers or pour lotas of milk which we've brought along into the spring. We have to step around a large man to do that. He sits praying in front of a stack of handwritten notes lit by a single diya. Something about him makes me believe he's been at this for a long time. But I know we are disturbing him by the frown that creases his forehead. At one point the Purohit steps around him and attempts to light a diya from the one illuminating the notebook. The man explodes wordlessly, hissing and waving him off like he would an irritating blue-bottle. The Purohit slinks off into his own corner without a peep and rummages in his pockets for matches. Just desserts, I think with some amusement. At the gates I had seen him bullying a small wretched looking man in a prayer cap and pheran. The same man who would later prove useful to me.

The puja ends with a dreadful rendition of Om Jai Jagdish Hare. I groan inwardly. I had been expecting a traditional Kashmiri Pandit hymn. I have *never* heard this bhajan being sung tunefully and the group here was being faithful to the tradition. "Om jay-aa-jag-a-deesh-a-hare-swaami-jayaa-jag-a deesh-hare," they squawked, dragging the tortured syllables painfully behind them. I grab the opportunity to slip away, and it is then that I realise that the pile of rags among the tins of ghee in one corner had a pair of round glasses, a flowing grey beard and a wide tooth-less smile.

"Come, sit," he says patting a sack into a seat. "Let's take a look at your hand."

I make myself comfortable and offer him my palms to read.

"Hmm," he growls disapprovingly, "Shani. Saturn rules. You married?"

"No."

"Good thing. But you should have, according to your hand, at twenty-eight."

He holds my palm close to his face. "What do you do?"

"I write..."

"Ah! Journalist. Silly profession. No integrity," he says the last in English. "According to your hand you should spend your life in spiritual activity."

"Join your profession?"

He throws back his head and laughs. "My profession, my *pro-fession*," he repeats, delighted with the joke. "I tell you, you're right, diksha and bheek, begging for alms is no longer what it was supposed to be but has become big business. When I first became a sadhu and hung out at the Kumbh I made a friend, an older sadhu. Everyday we used to step off the ghat into the river and then spend the rest of the time hanging out with the other sadhus smoking ganja at the akharas. One day my friend pointed at the sea of sadhus and spat in disgust, 'Look Rajen,' he said, 'mark them carefully. They are like the oil the halwai uses over and over again to fry pakoras, black and sour and without potency.'

Then I thought here I am a sadhu and I eat for free, but nothing is for free. I owe the universe."

Kumarji joins us and they greet each other effusively. "You've met Rajen Maharaj, I see," he says squatting besides me. The Purohit comes around with a platter, spots my forehead with a ver-milion tilak, pours dates and misri into Rajen Maharaj's lap and leaves the temple. His work is over for the day.

"Babaji is from Bengal and has been here for the last forty years," Kumarji tells me. I am intrigued. I thought I'd detected a Bengali accent and now try out my meagre store of Bengali on him. It is his turn to be delighted, and the Bengali seems to nudge a torrent of stories out of him. "I was at the Calcutta University very involved in student politics. CPI in those days, the undivided Communist Party of India. Before everything started to be divid-ed... Bengal, the Party, the country for God's sake! For years, even as a sadhu I was known as the Communist Sadhu. Tea... tea was wonderful then. We used to get Flowery Orange Pekoe at six Rupees a pound. Very good stuff, and we'd drink it like gentle-men, not like the sherbet they serve you in Kashmir. Pah! Came here in '58 after Amarnath but settled finally in '60. As I was telling you nothing is for free, so I started working. Cut grass every morning and went around from house to house feeding the cows..." he pauses. "Earlier it was the Hindu cows but after the

Pandits left, it was the Muslim cows." He collapses into laughter at his own joke.

"So, how come you came here, to Kashmir, to Khir Bhavani?"

He gives me a look, ignores my question and continues: "You see politics is supposed to serve the country, the people. But I soon realised that it was the politics of frustration. So I became a monk. Left the party and became a monk to serve people. Was in Belur Mutt for many years. Did you know Bose wanted to become a monk at Belur Mutt? No? Well, he did. And he was denied permission so he went on to form the INA. You think the British would've left without the INA? Hah! Gandhi and Nehru were all very well, but if it wasn't for Bose and the Indian National Army... Here, eat," he offers the dates.

"Why did I come here? Well, because of Swamiji. Swamiji inspired me. His life inspired me. And finally he chucked up everything because of the Devi right here" he says triumphantly.

"Er...which Swamiji?" I venture.

"Swami Vivekanand of course. Look, I don't believe in a personal God. Never have. Maybe because I was Communist or maybe because I became a Vedantist. All I know is that to concentrate the mind you need a personal God. I'm eighty-eight. I should know."

"And Swamiji..."

"Hmm. Swamiji had all sorts of plans and ventures, all kinds of ambitions before he came to Kashmir and stood before HER. One day standing right here—right here—in worship he thought: 'The Goddess has been manifesting in this wonderful place for centuries and when the Mohammedans came they destroyed her temple. Yet the people here did nothing to protect it.' The

Swamiji was thinking these thoughts, thinking if he was here he surely would have protected the temple. Just then, just as he was thinking these thoughts, a voice thundered in his head, 'Ho! Phellow!'" Babaji was jumping about his seat now, enacting the ancient drama vigorously, speaking in English "'Ho! The temple was destroyed because I *willed it so!*' it was the Divine Mother speaking," he whispered, eyes swimming large in his spectacles. "'If I wished I could live in a golden temple seven stories high but I prefer it this way. You phellow! *You will take care of me or I you?*'"

This, according to the Babaji prompted the Swami to take early retirement from proselytising.

"So, it doesn't matter?" I asked quietly, thinking of the all the ultimately useless acts of vengeance from the Babri Masjid to the ravaged temples of Kashmir.

"It doesn't. These are simply cycles..." He smiled, drawing a circle through the air with an arthritic finger.

The old ladies were fidgeting now and sighing meaningfully. It was time to go and I stood up reluctantly. "Babaji, what d'you think about Kashmir? I mean the situation, you've been here forty years…"

"You know how to make curd?"

"Well..."

"If you did then you'd know that you can't make sweet curd out of curd that is sour... Goodbye and bless you!"

I followed the old ladies out and waved goodbye to Babaji. The man with the notebook was still at prayer but he looked up and our eyes met. To my surprise his forehead unfurrowed and his face split into a beaming smile. I put my hands together and bowed slightly. He put his hand out in benediction and silently gestured that I should meet him the next time.

"Do you know that Sadhu, the one who doesn't speak?" I asked Kumarji at the gates as he struggled into his shoes.

"Which? Oh him! He's no ordinary Sadhu. Used to be a bureaucrat and a film maker. Quite high up in Doordarshan. Then he retired and came here. He's highly educated."

✛

4. The Sanctum sanctorum

Khir Bhavani, at 74° 48' long. 34° 13' lat., is an hour's drive north, just off the Srinagar-Leh highway. I found myself returning often, a warm feeling of homecoming suffusing me the moment the car crossed the churning clear waters of the Sind. Few people visit Khir Bhavani but the man selling flowers and incense is always at the gates, greeting me now with marked familiarity, shaking my hand and then touching his heart, "Aap theek hain? Aao chai piyo," he says.

Ghulam Mohammed Ganai looks like a villain with his thick mop of uncombed curls threaded with silver, the scraggly beard, one eye permanently closed, the other dancing behind grimy spectacles. But he's been here all his life, sitting at the Mother's feet, as he says.

Once, after I'd been inside he told me his story. His father had been the temple store keeper and after he died Ganai set up his stall outside the temple. That was seventeen years ago.

"Muslims don't come here after eating meat. You're not supposed to. It got so complicated, trying to figure out when I could and couldn't—if I ate at lunch that was it for the day and if I ate at dinner I couldn't come here in the evening as I usually do—that I turned vegetarian. On Eid this year my family had cooked a sumptuous meal and tried to persuade me to join them. And then I thought I'd have to stay away from Her if I did, so I didn't..." he explained, grinning lopsidedly.

"How are things here?" I asked.

"Quiet now. There weren't many boys who went from here across the border. The few who went were killed. Whosoever picks up the gun has to die," he said sagely. "There were some strange ones though," his voice dropped an octave. "Hubba. Joined the HM. He was a graduate. He'd even studied in Delhi. But he only lasted two years."

We are joined by Umar Butt, the caretaker of the temple for the last twenty-two years, the same small man whom I saw being bullied by the BSF Purohit on my first visit here. He salaams gracefully and squats on the earth next to us.

"And then of course there was Hamid," Ganai continued. "You know Hamid Gadda?"

"Yes."

"Well, Hamid was a drop-out, but he loved this place. As a child he used to run away from school, drop his books at the gates— right here—and spend the rest of the day singing bhajans. There used to be an old sadhu who died a few years ago. Hamid was his disciple."

I was intrigued by this place, by the relaxed, generous attitude of the Muslims, not to mention the Pandits, for I know of no other temple in India where there is a Muslim caretaker, where the gates are open to Muslims. Umar Butt, quietly listening all this while, now reads my thoughts. "Hum maante hain," he says emphatically. "We believe in this place. It's not simply that the Hindus believe and we think the idol is stone. No, we truly believe this is Bhagvati's place. We believe it is sacred. There is no cow slaughter in this village. You'll find Muslims coming here and offering milk to the spring just like the Hindus. "

"But the Jama'atis, don't they give you a hard time? They're constantly trying to separate pure Islam from what they consider corrupt?"

They both laugh. "The Jama'atis no longer strut around," says Umar Butt with surprising vehemence. "They're so terrified of being picked up by the army for their links with the Hizb that even the most righteous of them declare in writing that they have nothing to do with the organisation."

"And what about the spring?" I ask, aware of the legend that surrounds it.

"The spring is black now," Umar Butt sighs. "Once it was white and sometimes even a rosy pink. The first time I saw the waters turn black was in '84. I heard right after that Indira Gandhi had died and the Sikhs were being butchered in Delhi. Then it became black, pitch black, when militancy started, and then Kargil..." He lists the events slowly, carefully, making sure that he hasn't missed anything, "In '95 the waters became white again. Last month, though, they turned black. When things get bad, it is reflected in these waters."

✣

The days in Anantnag (literally, limitless spring) are soft as pashmina. The sun warms our skins with the gossamer lightness of shahtoosh.

Shafi Chaman is an artist who wears his vocation on his sleeve. *I am an Artist* says his bearing, his loping walk, his crooked smile, and people actually defer to him. We swagger down the streets in our pherans, ("In the early '90s it was Mast Gul and his cronies with their AKs walking up and down these very streets, my friend") past the copper shops and bakeries, past the shrine and the mosque. With him I feel we could be Cézanne and Monet. People here have an old-fashioned respect for artists. We drink endless cups of fine darjeeling tea while Shafi tells me about Ibn Batuta's travels in China as if it happened yesterday and Ibn was a pal. Later, we visit Mattan Nag. This has become ritual for us. Every time I visit Anantnag we must spend an hour or so at the waters of Mattan. Each time I am astounded by the blueness of the water tessellated by the mass of catfish speckled with gold, leaping, seething, moving as one, racing back and forth as we throw the puffed rice here and there, gleaming in the sunlight, glittering. Nishan claps her hands in delight, gurgling and dribbling in her father's arms. Her mother, a Raquel Welch lookalike is with Jaana, Shafi's mother, circumambulating the spring and then standing respectfully in front of the temple; both women, heads bowed, hands folded, looking like devout Pandit women at prayer. The whole scene is suffused with a noble and sublime indifference to the fact that these are Muslims at a Hindu Shrine. These are simply people in love with doing what they had done all their lives.

Water, spring, rock, cave, tree, mountain—all these are honoured, held sacred in Kashmir by Pandit and Muslim alike and imbued with the moving spirit. In truth their differences are on the surface. Deeper down they are animists, faithfully following

23

the traditions of their common ancestors. In Kashmir you can't take a step without walking into a shrine or temple built along a crevice, under a tree, over a spring. Great islands of peace in these turbulent times. Shafi points to one right near the house, behind the Masjid Sharif of Baba Dawood Khaki. The great Baba's descendent, the Imam of the mosque, leads the way with a great bunch of keys.

The Sharika Devi Bal spring is tiny, the mandir built over it is the size of a small box room, but it was of great significance to the Pandits of Anantnag. The door swings open with a creak. I peer in. It is desolate, abandoned, a few wan pictures of the Goddess still grace the walls. The spring oozes black filth onto the marble floor. An old rusted pump lies abandoned in one corner.

"Our women come now and then to clean but there isn't much they can do about the water," the Imam says apologetically. "I informed Pyare Lal Handoo when he came here last year, but you know what the government's like."

I approach the spring and look in: opaque—like looking into a dead man's eyes.

"The waters turned black in the winter of '88-'89 and over-flowed. The last time that happened was fifty years ago and then we had the plague which killed thousands, " he continued solemnly.

"And how it overflowed," Shafi recalled. " It ran past my house. The Pandits grew afraid. Some spoke of disaster and wanted to leave right then. It alarmed us all actually. We all felt something terrible was going to happen."

✛

Name: **Tika Lal Taploo**. Fathers Name: Pandit Nand Lal Taploo. Born: 6th Oct, 1927. Killed: 14th September,1989. Residence: Chinkral Mohalla, Habba Kadal, Srinagar. Survived by Wife (50), Sons (24, 21), Daughter (27). Name: **Ajay Kapoor**. Father's Name: Shiva Nath Kapoor. Born: 16.7.1940. Killed: 1.12.1989. Residence: Old Post office, Sr. Gunj Srinagar. Survived by wife (47), son (25), daughter (15). Name: **Sheela Koul** (Tiku) Husband's Name: Pran Nath Tiku. Born: December 1942. Killed: 31.10.1989. Residence: Dalhasanyar, Srinagar. Name: **Prem Nath Bhat.** Father's Name: Laxman Ji Bhat. Born: 5.12.1932. Killed: 27.12.1989. Residence: Anantnag. Survived by wife (52), sons (42, 38), daughter (31). Name: **Sarwanand Koul** **"Premi"** (Poet) and **Virendra Koul** (Son). Father's Name: Gopi Nath Koul. Born:9.6.1926/4.5.1962. Killed:30.4.1990. Residence: Sofshalli, Anantnag . Survived by wife (60), son (35), daughter (26) Name: **Bansi Lal Sapru.** Father's Name: Keshav Nath Sapru Born: 30.2.1945 Killed: 24.4.1990. Residence: Gulab Bagh, Srinagar. Survived by wife (37), Sons (16 and 13) Name: **Radha Krishen Kaw**. Father's Name: Balbhadher Kaw. Born: 18.5.1931. Killed: 24.8.1990. Residence: Kralkhud, Srinagar. Survived by wife (54), mother (75), daughter (35), son (3).Name: **Ashwani Kumar Garyali.**Father's Name: Shamboo Nath Garyali. Born: 23.4.1965.Killed: 24.6.1990. Residence: Chattabal, Srinagar. Survived by father (70), mother (60), brother (26), sister (22). Name: **Pushker Nath Razdan.** Father's Name: Tika Lal Razdan. Born: 18.3.1943. Killed: 12.10.1990. Residence: Khonmuha, Pulwama .Survived by wife (43), sons (23,20), daughter (16).Name: **Makhan Lal Raina.** Father's Name: Gopi Nath Raina. Born: 23.3.1938.Killed: 22.6.1990. Residence: Khanyar,

Srinagar. Survived by wife (42), daughter (22), son (20), father
(80), mother (68) Name: **Chand Ji Kher.** Father's Name: Dina
Nath Kher. Born: 2.3.1972. Killed: 17.7.1990. Residence: Vessu,
Anantnag. Survived by mother (55), sister (35). Name: **Raj Nath
Dhar.** Father's Name: Dina Nath Dhar. Born: 7.8.1931. Killed:
30.6.1990. Residence: Qutub-ub-din pore, Alikadal, Srinagar.
Survived by mother (70), sister (40), brother (32). Name: **Zinda
Lal Pandita.** Father's Name: Prakash Ram Pandita. Born:
4.4.1931. Killed: 6.10.1990. Residence: Bagatpora, Handwara.
Survived by wife (50), son (30). Name: **Jagar Nath Pandita.**
Father's Name: Ganesh Das Pandita. Born: 17.11.1943, Killed:
7.10.1990. Residence: Bagatpora, Handwara. Survived by mother
(62), sons (23 and 20). Name: **Omkar Nath Wali.** Father's Name:
Parmanand Wali. Born: 4.5.1935. Killed: 2.1.1991. Residence:
Chak-i-Rajwati, Vessu, Anantnag. Survived by wife (50), son (28),
daughters (24 and 22). Name: **Kanya Lal Peshin.** Father's
Name: Kanth Ram Peshin. Born: 4.10.1937. Killed:
18/19.10.1991. Residence: Pazalpora, Bandipora. Survived by
wife (48), sons (24 and 18), daughter (16). Name: **Gopi Nath
Raina.** Father's Name: Govind Ram Raina. Born: 1.1.1941.
Killed: 7.7.1990. Residence: Manigam, Ganderbal. Survived by
wife (45), daughters (28,20,17,15,12). Name: **Ashok Kumar
Bazaz.** Father's Name: Ram Joo Bazaz. Born: not known. Killed:
not known. Residence: Baghi Sunder Balla Chaṭṭabal. Survived
by wife and seven daughters (19,16,13,11,7,5,3). Name: **Pitti
Koul.** Husband's Name: Makhan Lal Koul. Born: 1.3.1938.
Killed: 7.11.1990. Residence: Mandir Bagh, Srinagar. Survived by
husband (53), son (26), daughters (28),mother (70). Name:
Maheshwar Nath Bhat. Father's Name: Zana Bhat. Born:

20.6.1921. Killed: 15.10.1990. Residence: Hazuri Bagh, Srinagar. Survived by wife (65), son (35), daughters (30,27,24) Name: **Shiban Kishen Koul.** Father's Name: Radha Krishen Koul. Born:13.5.1953. Killed:15/16.7.1990. Residence: Ashmuji, Kulgam, Anantnag. Survived by wife (35), mother (55), son (15), daughter (13). Name: **Girija Kumari Tiku.**Husband's Name: Kanya Lal Tiku. Born: 15.2.1969. Killed: 11.6.1990. Residence: Arigam, Bandipora. Survived by mother (60), husband (25), son and daughter (4 and 2) Name: **Dilip Kumar.** Father's Name: Mohan Lal. Born: 8.7.1962. Killed: 19.5.1990 Residence: Mujamarag, Shopian. Survived by mother (55), brothers (26,18,15).Name: **Manmohan Bachloo.** Father's Name: Janki Nath Bachloo. Born: 5.12.1963. Killed: 18.5.1990. Residence: Qazihama, Baramulla.Survived by Father (67), mother (56), sisters (25,23,19). Name: **Usha Kumari Koul.**Husband's Name: Rathinder Koul. Born: 13.6.1949.Killed: 14.10.1990. Residence: Sehyar, Ali Kadal, Srinagar. Survived by father-in-law (79), mother-in-law (68) son (10) Name: **Veer Ji Bhat.** Father's Name: D.N.Bhat. Born: 31.1.59. Killed: 13.5.1990 Residence: Nagam, Badgam. Survived by wife (30), daughter (5), son (3), father (60), mother (58). Name: **Ashok Kumar.** Father's Name: Basker Nath. Born: 2.5.1963. Killed: 13.5.1990. Residence: Pulwama. Survived by father (55), mother (54), sisters (30 and 24) Name: **Sarla Bhat.** Fathers Name: Shamboo Nath Bhat. Born: 30.9.1966. Killed: 18/19.4.1990. Residence: New Qazi Bagh, Anantnag. Survived by father (53), mother (48), brothers (26,18), sister (21). Name: **Surinder Kumar Raina.** Father's Name: Jia Lal Raina. Born: 19.3.1967. Killed: 2.5.1990. Residence: Tullamulla, Ganderbal. Survived by sisters (35,21), brothers (27,14) Name: **K.L.**

Ganjoo/Prana Ganjoo (wife) Father's Name: N.N. Ganjoo. Born: 4.1.1942/ unknown. Killed: 4.11.1990. Residence: Sopore. Survived by son (6), daughter (8). Name: **Surinder Kumar Koul.** Father's Name: Som Nath Koul. Born: 4.5.1971. Killed: 26.8.1991. Residence: Batagund, Handwara. Survived by father (50), mother (45), brother (30), sister (33). Name: **Ravinder Kumar Pandita.** Father's Name: Nanak Chand Pandita. Born: 4.10.1958. Killed: 25.4.1990. Residence: Mattan, Anantnag. Survived by wife (30), mother (60), daughters (4,6,6) Name: **Bushan Lal Koul.** Father's Name: Shridhar Koul. Born: 14.6.1948. Killed: 16.5.1990. Residence: Amnoo, Kulagam, Anantnag. Survived by wife (37), son (19) Name: **D.P. Khazanchi.** Father's Name: Damodar Khazanchi. Born: 6.10.1939. Killed: 6.10.90. Residence: Kaniya Kadal, Srinagar. Survived by wife (48), son (22), daughter (18). Name: **Prana Ganjoo.** Husband's Name: Jawahar Lal Ganjoo. Born: 10.4.1945. Killed: 17.6.1990. Residence: Malapora, Habakadal Srinagar. Survived by son (27), daughters (30,25,19). Name: **Durga Koul.** Husband's Name: Badri Nath Koul. Born: 8.10.1934. Killed: 17.6.1990. Residence: Malapora, HabbaKadal Srinagar. Survived by mother (75) son (30), daughter (28)[2].

These are just a few of the names of the Pandits who were killed by the militants between 1989-1991. I'd have to add some nine hundred more for you to get the complete picture. These women and men were not killed in the cross-fire, accidentally, but were systematically and brutally targeted. Many of the women were gang-raped before they were killed. One woman was bisected by a mill saw. The bodies of the men bore marks of torture. Death by strangulation, hanging, amputations, the gouging of eyes, were not uncommon. Often their bodies were dumped with notes forbidding anyone—on pain of death—to touch them. 900 brutal killings out of population of around 350,000 Pandits over a period of 24 months is a startling figure. Anyone who says Jagmohan engineered the Pandit exodus is a liar.

April 26, 1990: a press release of the JKLF from Rawalpindi, trying to distance itself from the killings of the Vice-Chancellor of the Kashmir University and his secretary, both Muslims, stated: "The JKLF wants to clarify its position... it might occasionally become necessary to organise operations like kidnapping and execution of hostages, hijacking, etc., the targets should be government officials and collaborators, not sons and daughters of the soil..."[3]

But who decides who is a collaborator and who a genuine son or daughter of the soil? The judge and the executioner together were born in anybody who picked up the AK47. When the Pandits fled, the sights were set on the Muslim populace. In a grim twist of fate the JKLF suddenly found themselves dislodged and hounded by other Mujahideen groups, hunted in turn like rabbits and killed mercilessly in the warrens of Srinagar's mohallas. Suddenly people were being murdered by shadowy assassins for no apparent reason: a family butchered in their kitchen as they ate dinner; a primary schoolteacher wiped out even as he taught, sitting under a beautiful young chinar; a poet in his eighties, ill and infirm, killed in his death bed; a university professor dragged out of class, tied to a tree and shot dead... Wandhama, Telwani, Sangrampora, Chittisinghpora... *Senseless violence* is a phrase which takes on new and hitherto unsuspected dimensions in Kashmir.

✧

"No, my name's not Gadda, it's Butt. Ghulam Mohammed Butt. Gadda was a name the security forces gave him." The speaker looked like the quintessential Kashmiri peasant: tall, lean, broad-shouldered, a prayer cap pushed to the back of the head, a waist-coat over the kameez, the shalwar hitched up above the ankles, enormous feet, hands like shovels.

"You see, he eluded them for eleven years. He was very smart, very resourceful. Once, when he'd just become a militant, he was caught in a cordon-and-search operation. There were so many of them closing in on him so he dived into the water and swimming underwater he reached the reeds. And there he stayed for seven hours—in that freezing cold water—breathing through a pipe he'd made from the reeds," Ghulam Mohammed said with restrained paternal pride, "That's why they named him Gadda."

Gadda. Hamid Gadda. Hamid the Fish: slippery as an eel.

His house was just a few hundred yards from Khir Bhavani, close enough to persuade Umar Butt, the caretaker, to sneak me past the BSF bunker to meet the family. Gadda's brother was waiting for us in front of the tiny two-storeyed house, nodding a curt greeting. It stood at the edge of the Gangkhai canal, now wide and green, moving slowly between dark banks pitted by the hooves of animals. I had been surprised by the size of the house: a small kitchen below and the room above it that served both as bedroom and living room for the family of six. Obviously, Hamid the Fish didn't make money out of militancy, or if he did he didn't send any home. But that was no reason for any want in hospitality, and soon we were served large glasses of hot milk and plates of biscuits. A few old blankets were quickly pulled out to cover our knees. Cushions were plumped and stuffed between us and the walls. I found myself deeply moved by all the fuss.

Once I had stopped Habla Bano, Gadda's mother, from retiring to the kitchen, she took over from her husband and spoke with remarkable confidence. I was struck by her open, relaxed face. She didn't look like someone who had lost her first born only a few months earlier. It was only later that I realised he had died so often in her imagination in the last decade, that she had wept so much in the early years, that the actual event so many years later had been a banal formality, and her own response as empty and perhaps even tinged with some relief.

"It was because of the mandir," she said smiling wistfully, "all because of Khir Bhavani." And then she told their story as the shadows lengthened in the courtyard below.

Autumn 1989. Gadda had just finished his dinner. It was harvest time. He'd worked hard in the fields all day, but there was still time enough for a quick visit to the temple. In the lane outside the house he came upon a knot of men, some armed. A few he recognised from a nearby village. They belonged to the Al Umar Commandos. When they struck up conversation with him, he realised to his horror that the plan was to blow up the temple. He tried reasoning with them and, when that didn't work, an argument and scuffle followed. Gadda was a big man, capable of taking on the whole bunch. They panicked and ran, leaving behind the gun he had snatched during the scuffle. He didn't know what to do with it so he took it along to the nearest Central Reserve Police Force (CRPF) bunker and handed it over to them. Then he made his way to the temple.

"But they were so angry, these Al Umar thugs," Habla Bano recalled, "that Hamid had to hide from them for days. They came looking for him, threatening all of us. We went to the police, the CRPF for protection but no one helped us. One day when he returned, the Al Umar got to know in no time and they swooped down on us and started dragging Hamid away. My husband wasn't around. I ran behind them crying, falling at their feet, begging them to spare him and take me instead. It was crazy, all these men with guns and me screaming, 'Shoot me! Kill me but spare him!' and Hamid struggling against six, seven of them bellowing, 'Don't touch her! Kill me, but leave my mother!' The CRPF bunker was so close, just across the canal. They did nothing. There must've been about thirty people watching quietly from their homes. They did nothing. I realised at that moment that we were alone, completely alone in this thing. They took us both but left me behind outside the village."

The ransom was the price of the AK47. When Gadda's father returned he set about selling a kanal of the little land he had. With only fifteen of the forty thousand that they had demanded in hand he tried to bargain for his son's life. They released him after the Hizbul Mujahideen, who had been approached by a relative, stepped in and persuaded them to do so.

"But it doesn't end there," said Habla Bano, rising to serve us biscuits, "they came back after a few weeks demanding the rest of the money, threatening us, waving their guns in our faces. We were so scared. Hamid worked as a weaver. He was a master weaver at a loom, an excellent weaver, but he couldn't dream of raising that sum in such a short while. The trips to the police and CRPF yielded no results. It was when Hamid went to the Hizb for help that they struck a deal. They would protect us if Hamid joined up. It was a horrible moment."

Hamid Butt went across the border and trained for six months. Then he crossed over and became Hamid Gadda, code name Bambar Khan. The Hizbul Mujahideen were true to their word and protected the family from the Al Umar Commandos, but there was little they could do about the raids of the security forces.

"For eight years the family slept separately, rotating between friends, relatives and neighbours every night, so that if we were picked up or killed the entire family wouldn't be wiped out in a stroke," said Ghulam Mohammed, taking up the tale. "It was so terrible. We used to live down river. This here used to be a cow shed. But our home was destroyed one night, blasted apart in '96."

"By whom?"

"Who knows? Thank God we weren't there that night."

"It all started because of the temple," Ghulam Mohammed frowned, looking for answers in his upturned palms. "You know I've devoted my life to it. I'm a karamchari. I clean the temple and don't take a pie for it. I don't know what sins we are paying for..."

A long silence settled between us and then Umar Butt, the caretaker, tapped his wrist. "We better leave now," he said worriedly, "we'll all get into trouble..."

"Often I'd hear of big militants surrendering," Ghulam Mohammed suddenly said, "and my heart would leap up with the possibility... I would send word to Hamid, sometimes even go and see him myself and beg him to surrender. This is a dog's life, I would say to him, for you and for us. Give it up, I would plead. But he was a changed man: Didn't listen.

"Then in '96, during the elections, the renegades picked me up one day and took me to the polling booth. You know how it is during the elections, with the militants doing everything to scare people away and the government forcing the people to vote. Well, these guys were the pro-government Ikhwan. Kuka Parrey's men. They stripped me naked and made me stand in front as a shield saying if Hamid Gadda attacks the booth he'll have to kill his father first. The security forces just stood by and watched the scene. They were twenty: I was alone. Then half way through the polling, someone did open fire. Five people were shot. Two killed. I was lucky," he said rolling up his sleeve to show a dark scar running from his shoulder down the withered bicep to his forearm. "I got away with just this."

"Who...?"

"Don't know... maybe Hamid's men, maybe someone else..." I stared dumbly at him. He wasn't ruling out the possibility of his son pulling the trigger on him. Umar Butt tugged at my sleeve insistently. "We must go. This is too risky."

I stood up and took my leave, thanking the gracious family. Habla Bano hugged me and showered kisses on my cheeks and forehead. "Come back soon," she said smiling.

Then Ghulam Mohammed took my hand and thanked me. "No, no, thank you, takleef muaaf," I had said, feeling acutely embarrassed. Gadda's sisters stood at the door, giggling shyly.

"What's your name?" I asked Gadda's brother as he bade me farewell.

"Fayaz Ahmed Butt."

"What do you do?"

"Nothing now, but I used to be an SPO."

I was shocked. "How were you a Special Police Officer? What about your brother?"

He smiled. "We didn't get along after he became a militant. I didn't want him to become one. Then later when I joined the police he sent messages threatening me," he shook his head. "He once even put out a contract on my head. And then the police would hassle me. Never trusted me. Where's your brother? How should I know, I'd tell them, I hate him. But they didn't believe me and it got too much so I chucked it up."

We stared at each other a long while. Then I asked, "Well, what would you like to do now?"

His eyes lit up. "Join the police, of course."

✣

5. The Gates

He held the blue box up to the light, twirling it slowly as one would a precious jewel, reading: "LOP...CHUUU.... Phhlowery... Orange...Pekoe.. Bahh, Bhalo! Wonderful!"

"Happy Diwali, Babaji."

"Oh aaj ke Kali Pujo? Then Happy Diwali to you, too."

I had looked for him all over. He wasn't among his pile of ghee tins in the pavilion and I was starting to worry when I saw a bundle of rags and a wooden staff under a chinar. I noticed his feet were covered by a pair of cloth shoes he'd obviously made for himself and those together with his patchwork gown made him look like an ancient druid. He lay happily in the dappled sunlight, gnarled hands folded across his chest, chewing cud the way very old people tend to do.

"But you better take this back and drink it for me. There's no one here to make it, and I'm too old to do it myself."

I start to insist, calling a BSF jawaan from the kitchen at the back and explaining how to make a decent brew, when the silent meditator appears. The fierce one. We greet each other. He ignores my namaste and embraces me, thumping the wind out of my lungs at the same time.

He gesticulates frantically, pulling me behind him back to the Babaji. I give him my notebook and pen so that I can understand him better. *Don't bother about the tea. Take it back. There's no point. He has no SELF,* he writes in English.

I smile, shrugging my shoulders. "My name's Sonia. When is your penance, your maun vrat over, I'd like to talk to you?"

In another month.

The Babaji stirs, opens an eye and says, "Don't talk to him. He's a Pandit. All Pandits are rakshasas, ogres of the highest order."

The man throws back his head and laughs silently. Then he snatches the notebook and writes for a long time before handing it back for me to read.

My name is SWAMINATRI. I was a press correspondent. Worked for local papers and some foreign papers & lastly UNI. Then I went to the Film and T.V. Inst. Won international award for my film, 'Never on a Sunday.' Worked for some time in Bombay. Then joined TV, working as ASD News Doordarshan Directorate, Mandi House. I am still a member of the Press Club.

P.S. After retirement facing the odd circumstances here in

Kashmir I am now devoted to 'Mother'.

I look up from the notebook and find him beaming at me. I can't wait to hear the whole story.

"Do you know why there is no peace in Kashmir, Sonia?" Babaji suddenly asks.

"Well, I guess because of intransigent attitudes, no one wants to give an inch..." I venture.

"No. The deeper reason?"

I invite him to continue by keeping quiet. I know he's dying to tell me.

"Because this is Kali and Bhairav's place!" he says triumphantly. "Vishnu. Now the places that belong to Vishnu are more or less peaceful, but this belongs to Kali and to Shankar, to Mahakal. There have to be cycles of destruction. Shankarji's dancing the tandav now, and the waters turn black. The Goddess is upset, the waters turn black. But one day, you'll see, the waters will clear. You'll see."

We look instinctively towards the little shrine in the murky waters. There among the yellow and orange marigolds, on the head of the Goddess perch a pair of exquisite Himalayan bulbuls. I laugh aloud with delight. This is miracle enough, this place: the Gangkhai, this courtyard with the enormous chinars, the clouded spring, the wonderful old men, and now the birds.

"What's the time?" Babaji props himself suddenly on a frail elbow.

"A quarter to one."

He leaps up with amazing alacrity and gathers his things.

"What's wrong Babaji? Where are you going?"

"I'm late. It started at 12:30."

"What? What's started...?" I cry out after the swiftly receding figure dodging behind the trees.

Just then a sudden gust of wind sussurated among the leaves of the great chinars so that the voice that came back was tiny and broken, but I could've sworn it sounded like: "My... fav...ouritetee... veepr..ogramme.... Nev...ermissit...."

6. The Path

It is autumn and I'm hovering somewhere between the 9th and 14th centuries, recovering some of Kashmir's rich past in my explorations of ancient sites and still more ancient people—amateur historians, mythologists, anchorites, all. It is truly fascinating and far more engaging than the dreadful accounting of killings and tortures that has occupied me all year. The weather is gorgeous. Brilliant sunshine and a cold that nips pleasurably. The gigantic chinars and poplars are turning to rust and gold. Great flocks of sheep and long-haired goats swarm down from the high pastures, flooding the plains, drowning the highways so that even now, on this road to Ganderbal....

1. Samsar Chand Koul, *Srinagar and its Environs,* Third Edition, Mysore 1962

2. Excerpted from Mohan Lal Koul, *Kashmir, Wail of a Valley,* Delhi 1999 Part 2, Chapter 8.

3. *Kashmir Under Siege: Human Rights in India,* Asia Watch, New York, May 1991, fn 166 p. 131

MINA KUMAR

Reading

THIS IS THE STORY of a young relative of mine, Anjolie, and how I came to provide her some assistance, after a fashion, in an hour of need. The question of what do about Anjolie has been a recurring one within our family, ever since her mother, my cousin, died fifteen years ago, thus confounding everyone's expectation that she would continue to motivate gossip for many years to come. My cousin's daughter, conveniently enough, took her mother's place in fueling conversation in those nights when blackouts meant there was nothing to do but sit in the verandah (men), on the roof (young and middle-aged women), or in Paati's bedroom (the most senior women), and discuss the happenings of the day.

My mother, a great beauty in her youth who had married a very wealthy man, had a happy marriage, and a reasonably good, if somewhat distant, relationship with her children. If there was some store of personability and likeability in the family, it had all been issued to my mother, as inheritances of jewellery are sometimes divided by stone. The others received financial acumen or singing ability or culinary expertise, and intractable, difficult personalities which made any social gathering occasions for conducting prolix or subtle feuds. I remember scenes of happiness, but they were invariably solitary: Paati in the kitchen, expressing her more tender emotions through the application of copious amounts of ghee; Indira tending to her rose plants with lavish compliments to their blossoms; my uncle watching over his Doberman pinschers as they ate their noontime meal of thayir satham and left-over poriyal, his moustachioed face contorted with concern for their good health. If it hadn't been for my mother and father and their coy romantic gestures, I would never have imagined that other people could be a source of comfort and solace. I suspect that even their affection for us was due to our embodiment of their romantic relations—"Savitri, you have given me two sons and a lovely daughter," my father would boom as he presented her with New Year or Deepavali silk saris, and my mother would blush and absent-mindedly pat the head of the nearest of their offspring.

If the others in the family took any lesson from my mother's happiness, it was that women are made sweet-tongued and companionate by gifts of expensive saris—a lesson unfortunately not borne out by the relations of either of my brothers with their wives. The sources of happiness were a much-debated topic in our family, and the invariable conclusions—it is best to want nothing, feel nothing, act out of duty, leave all in the hands of God, desire only the opportunity to visit holy places in one's old age (female); it is best to make lots of money, hoe one's own row and avoid entanglements with others (male)—were clearly somehow inadequate, insufficient. There was close scrutiny of other family members to see if they had somehow managed the trick of being happy.

My paati, who had thick white (later yellowy) hair to her hips for forty years of widowhood, whose father had sported a moustache and educated all of his eight daughters, who allowed my mother some veto over the selection of a groom ("There's no need for the galata of suicide, if you would kill yourself just tell me now," she told my mother), was not entirely opposed to modern ways, but she believed in prudence and careful evaluation of the available facts: hence the interest in the outcomes of other people's lives. Anjolie's mother had divorced Anjolie's father because he spent too much time with his work and gave her too little attention: a novel complaint. The women in my family liked men to stay in their place—Paati did not bother to hide that she found her widowhood more pleasant than her marriage. It was testament to the uniqueness of my parents' relationship that they would sit together in the evenings (him reading the newspapers, her mending clothes or sitting idly, flies buzzing around the fluorescent light), and she did not find his company nerve-wracking or onerous. Anjolie's mother's subsequent experiences reinforced familial wisdom: she married a poorer man who gave her his undivided attention—that is to say, she was obliged to endure the full force of his idiocy—and had to divorce him, too. Happily, she was killed in a train crash before the second divorce went through, who knows what would have happened to her afterwards—all this because of her unreasonable expectations of male usefulness! It was a warning given to all the women of marriageable age, and given to all the mothers of grooms. Gossip was my family's way of publishing the results of individual experiments, and this is why, as the mother of two girls, I came to know a great deal of the story of Anjolie.

The essence of my family, to me, is a story my uncle told me about his grandfather. My great-grandfather had been sent, as an old man, to the wedding of his great-niece in some village in Kerala. He had been put on the train, and received in the village, then put back on the train after the wedding ceremonies were over. The poor, doddering old man, however, never made it back to the city, and was never found—no one knew what happened to him. I heard this story when I was ten or eleven, and was shocked. "Oh, he wanted to go alone, I am sure of it," said my uncle. There it is—the carelessness, the indifference to expectations of sentiment, the disinterest, the acceptance of loneliness.

On her father's side, Anjolie had a different inheritance. My predominant impression of her father's relatives is their ugliness—except for the eldest of his brothers, her father and his siblings were strikingly unsightly. They were almost Iyerish in their crudeness, though they had their pretensions: I recall one of Anjolie's aunts thrusting upon me cassettes of her grandfather declaiming Shakespeare. Perhaps it is only that my family is composed of individuals, whereas Anjolie's father's family came in a clump. The siblings were famously close-knit—Anjolie's mother told me she longed to join them for that very reason, to be embraced by their familial warmth. But they had something we did not have. If one of us wrote horrid poetry or told tall tales of his experiences or committed complex financial crimes, he would have been mocked and excoriated and subject to the full weight of our wit and contempt. They, on the other hand, were loyal above

all, admiring the poetry, seconding the stories, denying the impro-
priety. If Anjolie's father was a remarkably indifferent parent, we
were no better, but in his family, they lauded his affections.
Clumped above all. And Anjolie's mother, quick-witted and given
to reading Byron after dinner, incapable of staying her tongue,
found it impossible to give what she had to give in order to be
clumped.

My own feeling for Anjolie, whom I have known since she was a
chubby, crop-haired girl, is I think what Indira felt for me, when
she tried to teach me to garden. I was thirteen, and not interested,
a budding feminist who wanted out of the garden and kitchen, and
out to the verandah, out to the world. Her lectures on the proper
care of rose bushes and lime trees were not as much fun as inviting
myself to sit with the men and offering my opinions of Annadurai
and Kamaraj. My indifference to Indira's instruction made me
circumspect in offering Anjolie advice when she was younger, and
in any case, I was in Fiji in the time of her worst troubles. And yet,
as our family withered away—for we had few children, and my
mother's three and my two made us conspicuously fertile in our
respective generations—I sometimes wondered what it was that
could be done for her.

When I was offered a one-semester visiting lecturer position at an American university, I thought it would be good for my
career, and an interesting research opportunity, but I had some
trepidation about leaving my young girls. My husband was good
for Sunday ice-cream treats, and would take them swimming if
they asked, but not much more. Did they really need me to question their food intake and enforce the completion of all assigned
homework? They were not demonstrative girls, happily scribbling

in drawing pads behind closed doors. When I asked if they would mind me going away for four months to America, they asked only if I would buy them nice foreign clothes, one wanting a riding habit she had seen illustrated in *Vogue*. My husband minded most, thinking that there was something unsuitable about his wife jetting off to foreign lands, but I described the wonders it would do for my research and he relented. He is a scientist, and holds pure research above the opinions of his family. When I ran into an aunt of Anjolie's at Woodlands, as I averted my eyes from the huge blobbed birthmark on her forehead, and told her of my plans, she remarked that Anjolie was attending the same university.

I arrived at the university in the end of August. It was my second extended stay abroad. I had visited America once before to stay with my husband's brother and his family in Texas: my husband spent his time looking for a suitable employment opportunity, while I went golfing with his brother's wife. I had also lived in Fiji for a few years, while my husband worked on ecological research with an international environmental organization. My children were so young then, toddlers, so my own research was perhaps a little different from what I would have liked, but it was my Fiji work which obtained the position in America.

After moving into the university housing, I phoned Anjolie to see if she would like to join me in some coffee. I had not seen her since she was thirteen, two years before she had her worst trouble, and right before I went to Fiji. She had come to visit with a cousin, and had played cards with my husband as her cousin cooed over the babies and stuffed idli down their throats. When I phoned her, she seemed happy to hear from me, and agreed with enthusiasm to meet me at a cafe near the university.

The cafe was a large, unattractive place with a huge bar inside that apparently featured comedic performances as well as magic shows for children, and a smaller section outdoors. Anjolie had already arrived when I came, and I joined her outside, under a large umbrella. She had already ordered a glass of wine.

We sat in silence as I studied the menu, surreptitiously examining her. She was leaning her arm against the metal gate guarding the outdoor seating area, resting her head in her palm, a pose both classical and typical of her mother. She wasn't as fair as her mother nor as beautiful, a dark, blurry xerox of her mother's elegant features. Once she had longed to be more exotic, and experimented with telling strangers she was half-French or German. Although her mother had once been taken for Greek, and we had a distant Hebbar relative with hazel eyes, it was impossible to think of Anjolie as other than what she was. She had changed the spelling of her name in her half-French phase, no doubt having read in the papers of Anjolie Ela Menon—she had been plain Anjali before. Although this phase died, the Anjolie had stayed because her father, a man given to describing himself as Aryan, had written it down as such in her passport application.

I set the menu down, and looked at her frankly. She smiled at me with thickly-painted maroon lips, and said what I least expected: "I read your books, you know."

My first book, my Ph.D. thesis, was published by OUP. It is now perhaps the standard work on the effect of modern agricultural implements on village economies. The sequel is to be the definitive work on the effect of irrigation projects on the rural economy, a topic racy enough to generate much interest at OUP, but babies and Fiji temporarily distracted me. In any case, my first book was the only one in any significant distribution, and could have been a set text in a class Anjolie had taken.

My next book was on economic networks in Fiji, a more socio-logical work published by a local press in a limited run of cloth-bound, hand-sewn books full of misprints. They smelled lovely though. I could not imagine Anjolie had seen it, although the director of her university's Anthropology department had, which is why she wrote to tell me about the similar work she and two oth-ers were doing on networks in America, and the availability of the visiting lecturer position. A Punjabi gas station magnate in New Jersey had recently commanded a mafia-style execution of a col-league—it sent shivers of excitement through our small coterie.

"You read my books?" I said.

"Yeah, when I was at Rama Chiththi's house," she replied, brushing her hair out of her face. This I found even more puz-zling, as I could not imagine that lumpy Rama, with her stench of sweat and talcum powder, would be capable of reading *Femina,* much less the then recently-published *Modern Agricultural Implements and the Economy of Madras Presidency, 1880-1955.* Our food and drink ordered, as we waited for it to arrive, she told me how she came to read my books.

After her mother had died, Anjolie had lived with the family of first one and then another of her father's siblings, but finally, her father, who was working in Dubai, had her sent to an American boarding school about thirty miles from the cafe at which we sat. It was a school whose greatest pupils became the wives of diplo-mats or bankers, and were featured in the society pages, although it was not necessarily the first or second school they attended. Anjolie came back to her father's siblings for her summer vacations, but for the vacations within the school year, she was obliged to stay with the family of a friend of her father's. The family, needless to say, was not thrilled at this imposition, and Anjolie was temperamentally unsuited to the abnegation required of poor guests. Anjolie did her best to ingratiate herself with the schoolmates most likely to take to her, so that she might stay with them instead. This ingratiation led to her first troubles: the evasion of curfew, sneaking out at night to parties ("Not like Malory Towers at all," she told me), beer, the ganja roll. She was popular, but still, two weeks thrice a year was not nothing to ask of even the best of fellow ganja-smokers. She fell in love.

He was a black, this I knew. He was living with a woman in the town near her school, although she was not his wife. The woman was white, of Italian descent.

"Did you hear about all that happened?" Anjolie asked.

"Only why you came to stay with Rama," I replied.

She shrugged. One day, weeks later, we met in Queens after I had completed some fieldwork, and went to a Greek restaurant. As we ate, Anjolie told me all about this man and his "Gino" girlfriend, who had all the self-abnegation Anjolie did not have. Anjolie claimed he had liked her for her spiritedness. She even pulled a picture of him out of her purse. He had a fair, weak little face, like a Regency hero, with pouty pink lips and long, loose curls. I had imagined he would be less girlish, somehow. "For that guy to be my first love," she said. "His breath always tasted like vendakka from all the beer he drank." But on this first occasion, in the cafe, she said only that she had had a friend who let her stay in the apartment he shared with a woman.

Indira told me once, when I was young, that her mother had seen only one menstrual period before she became pregnant. We told each other we were glad to go to school instead of becoming wives so quickly, and we meant it, despite our natural longings—Anjolie's mother was in love with Darcy from *Pride and Prejudice*—because we were still so close to the lives behind us. We were the first generation of women to go to college, to have choices, and to choose what was in any case inevitable (marriage, babies) seemed pointless. Those were the limits of our thoughts.

Anjolie became pregnant. She forged invitations from the friend of her father's when she wanted to stay with this man, and did so again on the weekend she was scheduled for a termination at the local women's hospital. The one school-friend she told of her plans thought it wise to tell the administration of her condition and true whereabouts. Anjolie was in the apartment with him and the other woman when they knocked on the door. She panicked, went into the bathroom, and took all the aspirin in the medicine cabinet.

"They should have let you die." How many times had her father said this, and mangled-faced Uma, Rama and her husband? Her father had asked Uma to deal with this situation, seeing as it fell under the category of "female problems." Uma was recently married but childless, and since Anjolie's father had lent her husband the money to purchase their house, it was meet that she fulfill this mission. One of the first things Anjolie's mother told me about her new family was that Uma hoarded chocolates in her sari closet, and would sit in front of it in the evenings, masticating "discreetly" so she wouldn't have to share them. Thus had Uma acquired her reputation within her family for diplomacy.

Anjolie had a miscarriage. In the hospital, she was assigned a therapist, who would come in the afternoon and talk to Anjolie: "When did you start having suicidal feelings? How long have you wanted to kill yourself?" The man, fearful of being arrested for statutory rape, did not come, but sent her messages through schoolmates. She did not wish to leave the hospital, lying in bed watching cartoons all day, refusing to speak to Uma. Uma could say little, what with some stranger in the other bed in the room.

"I got pregnant, and then I tried to kill myself, you know, because I didn't want to deal with everyone screaming at me. I wanted to stay in the hospital forever. I begged the therapist not to let me go!" Anjolie laughed. "The therapist told Uma Chiththi, and we were like two steps out of the hospital when she spat on me." Anjolie made a face in imitation of Uma. "I had a big gob of spit on my face, and she was like, how could you beg them not to let me take you? How embarrassing was that for me? I had to grin in front of those white people and listen to this, pisas, pey, shenian. If it wasn't for your father, I would have thrown you in the garbage." Anjolie gave a quick, short exhalation. "Well, it was a long time ago." She finished her wine, and twirled the stem between her fingertips.

Our food arrived, and as the dishes were placed before us, Anjolie continued. "So I packed up and we went back to India. That's when I realized how completely I had messed up. There were these huge all-party conferences to decide who was going to put me up." Uma had only recently been married, Anjolie's eldest uncle had a teenage son as yet uncorrupted, Anjolie's second uncle's wife was a woman of delicate disposition (and significant personal wealth), Rama had a daughter of five or six, each sibling had some reason to decline. Anjolie's mother had no siblings, both of her maternal grandparents had passed away, and Paati was considered too old to be given the burden of her upkeep, so there seemed to be no way of her mother's family being given the responsibility. Her father interrupted his important business dealings to fly back and enter into these delicate negotiations, making Anjolie weep and beg each of his siblings and their spouses in turn for the opportunity to experience their mercy and benevolence. Finally, Rama's husband, who was notorious in my family for his many quixotic schemes, obliged Anjolie's father by allowing Anjolie to stay in his house in return for a small investment in his latest project, a factory which made leather puppets for the tourist market. "My father got so mad that he was having to shell out so much money because of me!" Anjolie said, laughing, her mouth glistening with avocado. "And I kept telling him, but I always got good grades, I was like a straight A student."

So many evenings, in my Paati's home, the women on the roof would mull the lessons of Anjolie. Was she an argument against boarding schools? Against divorce? Against foreign travel? And what could any of us do to instruct her out of the life that she was leading? My brothers and their families had taken her to lunch at the Chola, and Anjolie had made eyes at a white man at another table. Rama and my friend Jamini had seen each other in Pondy Bazaar, and as they talked, Anjolie had flirted with the nada seller. It was an embarrassment to take her outside the house, Rama had told Jamini. And Uma came upon her diary which was a torrid series of imagined scenes with the man she left behind, as well as others. She even had drawn—her mother was quite gifted at drawing, as are my own two girls—scenes of debauch. Even when she was younger, Anjolie had gotten into her grandfather's bookcase, to his copy of *Sex in History*—an absurd volume which speculated on Hans Christian Anderson's visits to prostitutes and similar items on other famous people—and announced her reading matter to all and sundry. Paati told my uncle to lock up his reference books (he claimed that this volume was necessary research for his duties as a lawyer, and kept it with his law journals). No one was surprised at what had befallen Anjolie, as no one was surprised that her mother, in love with Romantic poetry, would reject husbands because they were insufficiently devoted or because their devotions were expressed with insufficient brilliance. For reading matter too entered into the equation.

We knew that people could be spoilt by literature or scenes in movies. We, no less than eighteenth century European women who hid novels in their skirts and only read in the afternoon, thought there was something suggestive about reading non-religious literature. And yet, it was acknowledged by our elders that to read in English or French gave a patina of elegance, and even for girls, it was a risk worth taking. For our birthdays, we received bound volumes of Dickens and Dostoevsky, and our requests for more were greeted with good humor. I would instigate my brothers, who were bored by anything that involved sitting still, to request titles to augment my collection. As long as it was written many years ago, it was presumed safe, as were sewing, drawing and parcheesi.

"I was so bored at Rama Chiththi's, from the beginning I was writing letters to my teachers telling them that I had been such a good student and asking them to help me come back. There was just nothing to do." Anjolie sipped water and sat back, half her face in sunlight. She blinked her eyes. "I mean, if I stepped out of the house everyone came running to see what I was doing. There was no one to talk to, there was no watching TV. I mean even if there was something that wasn't like a documentary about European termites or something, Rama Auntie would be in front of it, or her mother-in-law, my god, who would like keep trying to get me to do simultaneous translation into Tamil, like of *Bringing Up Baby* or something, I just couldn't take it."

Anjolie was a corporeal ghost in the house. For her to mingle in the household was awkward, but for her to stay in her room like a paying guest was offensive. Rama did her best to include her: for the last twenty years, Rama has been attempting to lose weight, and she put Anjolie, who was chubby then, on a diet too, measuring out her rice and curry. That, and made her sit in the idol room and write "Sri Ramajayam" two hundred times each morning. On occasion, Anjolie visited her maternal Paati's house and ate her fill of paysam. When she was little, Paati would tell her stories of Rama and Narasimha, but there was no conversation now—Anjolie was at that awkward age in between Paati's interest in a child and a woman's interest in her paati. Anjolie's paternal cousins were at school, and had in any case been warned against her company. She had no friends of her own in the vicinity.

"I felt like was in solitary confinement," Anjolie said, maroon lips pursing. Our empty dishes were taken away and she ordered a sorbet for dessert. It was a mix of mango and lime flavours, and apparently a special delicacy of the establishment. "My god, I cried and cried and cried. I missed that guy, I missed my friends."

It was difficult for American youngsters to imagine the importance of letters, and in any case, there was something unpleasant about reading mail which had been vetted by Rama. After her diary was discovered by Uma—and thus the fact that she had stolen some money from a visiting relation of Rama's husband, and used it to buy a magazine and some sweets— there was no solace in writing. "I visited Rama Chiththi two years ago—my father forced me to—that was the last time I went to India—and I saw that she still had my diary in her room, even though she told me she was going to throw it away. I don't know what she's keeping it for."

What would you do with such a daughter, Indira wrote to me in Fiji, who lied, who forged signatures, who had smoked ganja, who had had sex, who had tried to kill herself, who stole money from your guests, at only fifteen? My eldest brother would have beaten her, as he beats his son. My second brother's wife would try psychology, which she studied in college. I told Indira that I did not know what I could or would do, that was the truth. In some ways her experience of the world was wider than mine even as an adult, much less at her age, and it made me hesitate to pronounce judgement. At least Anjolie settled one question: everyone saw that she was unhappy, and there were sighs of satisfaction from Madras to Pondicherry that the wages of sin were sorrow.

"I would have tried to kill myself again, but I was scared I'd botch it. My father swore to me that if I ever did that again he would send me to a mental home," said Anjolie. "Can you imagine an Indian mental hospital?" She shook her head. "I know I was lucky in a way. I mean, thirty years ago they would have killed me or thrown me in the street," she said. She pushed the dish of sorbet towards me so I could try it. I put my soup spoon in it and scooped some up. It was too cold for me to taste much else but sweet and tart, I could hardly tell it was mango.

"Thirty years ago, you probably would not have had the opportunity to get into the same trouble," I said.

"People didn't get lonely back then?" she asked me, her dark eyes luminous. "Or weren't selfish enough to care about their own feelings." She gave a laugh, and raised the dish of sorbet. "More cruel, please." She sat back, tilting her head to feel the sun, composing her face. It was the first sign of feeling she showed. "I guess only people who have their own money have any right to be happy."

I could illustrate this maxim with instances—my father flinging rice in my eldest brother's face, and saying, "As long as you're eating my rice... "; my uncle beating Indira's head against the wall because she came home from college wearing lipstick; Paati sitting in the kitchen with her three children to evade her husband's notice, that is to say wrath—and yet, my childhood had been happy, my mother had a happy marriage and wept for days when my father died, my daughters seemed happy...my housewife friend Jamini, doing ikebana in the afternoon, was content. My father raged over my brothers' educational short-comings, and insisted on choosing their courses of education, future occupations and even haircuts, but he was not an angry man, and would not be angry if he was not defied, which made him a father my brothers still commend. And my mother had little temper, and was rarely bothered as long as her children were quiet and within sight, unlike Anjolie's mother's mother, whose rage was sudden and all-consuming. We believed our elders had the right to limit our lives, as their lives were limited by their elders and their sense of propriety. Paati behaved as if she was leader of the supreme command, firmly monitoring the digestion and finances of her sons, but she herself lived in constant concern for the thoughts of her elder sisters and the mamis down the road. I disagreed vociferously with my mother over whether or not it was risqué to wear salwar-kameez, but my anger was diluted by my love for her, and her love for me, which sent her to the kitchen to make vadas with which to propitiate me when I was angry. Well-mannered parents, a well-mannered husband who encouraged me to continue my studies after we wed, I had no need for cynical maxims, except that I was a daughter of my family, and not given to averting my eyes.

"I did lots of stupid things," Anjolie conceded grandly, waving her long spoon about. "I could have been a lot smarter. I was honest to my diary, you know, which was like totally insane when Rama was reading my mail."

Anjolie was infamous for her self-possession: even in her unhappiness, Anjolie would mimic Rama's husband's English or snort at some misstatement of my eldest brother or raise her brows at Uma when she ran to give her husband his spectacles, without any sense that these were incitements. Worse, while our family had some latitude for such behaviour—that is, we found it wrong and worthy of punishment, but not astonishing—her father's family thought her behaviour obscene. She had no sense of gratitude, though they requested it of her. "Isn't my father paying you for this?" she had said to Rama, as Rama watched her eat an apple. This story spread like fire, I received four accounts of it in Fiji. They had excused her American imbroglio to keep her clumped, and she had no sense of compromising to be within their familial embrace. They did not dare ask for remorse, for she seemed no more conscious of her sins than a dog or a cat, and they had limits on what they were willing to do to try to remind her of her position. She was given food and water, a place to sleep, her needs were fulfilled, an animal in the house. An animal, at least, would wag its tail and lick your hands.

"But then, I found some happiness, because of you, Ambika Auntie," said Anjolie. She gave a large grin, brushing hair out of her face. Then she drank some water. "It's like the hidden benefit of class, or something like that, right? We're reading about that in one of my women's studies classes." She slurped some more water. "I was so miserable, you know, I was just so trapped and I couldn't see the way out. I couldn't go outside, there was no one to talk to and everybody was always getting pissed at me, so I just shut up, right. But what was there to do in my room? If they let me stay in my room. What was I going to do in the living room? I read all of Rama's comics in a week. I mean, worse come to worse, here you can go the library or the pool or something, and in India they wouldn't even let me get books from the American Centre, I don't even know what they were afraid of. It was just so awful. And if I said anything, Rama Chiththi would make me clean the cupboard or something. So anyway one day I was in Paati's house, and I just went up into the attic, you know, just to be alone and not have anyone come up to me. I was kind of looking around, not like I was snooping or anything like that, but the box was open, and that's how I found your books."

"I see. You read *my* books," I said, and perhaps I smiled.

"Yeah, she in darkest Africa, and pirates, and stuff," said

Anjolie. "I mean, I read the longer ones about everybody getting married because they took up so much time, they were fat, but the ones I really liked were the ones about people getting hacked up."

"Was that the appeal? People getting hacked up?"

"Sometimes it was," she said, emphatically. "*She* was pretty racist though."

"I don't think I noticed. Or perhaps it just didn't strike me as remarkable."

"Yeah, so like nothing is ever remarkable, right?" Anjolie pushed her dish aside. "This is exactly what I hate so much. Like everything is the way it is and that's it. It's like I'd say something was unfair, and they'd be like, oh, everything happens for the best, and I was like, come on, you know, like *The Lisbon Earthquake* was like how many years ago. I'm so glad I'm not there any more."

I had been told *The Lisbon Earthquake* story too while still in Fiji. Anjolie had mentioned it to Rama's mother-in-law in some arch dismissal of the old woman's piety, and her uncle had hit her so hard that one side of her face had bruised to a dark purple. Anjolie had insisted on calling her father immediately to tell him what had happened to her. Her father in Dubai, aroused out of his bed, had wept that he would die from the strain of apologizing for her to all of his brothers and sisters. Wept or screamed or raged, depending on the version.

"So Rama goes, oh, we only put up with you because of your father. And I was like, why do you think I put up with you? It's only because I don't have anywhere else to go. Do you think I *want* to be here? Then I'd go read a nice storybook with people stabbing each other. That was about as wholesome as I got, read-ing 'classic literature.'" She mimicked Rama's husband's lisp.

"Why did they have to make life so awful?"

"Perhaps they ask the same thing about you, Anjolie." She glared, her lashes looking especially dark and sharp as her eyes widened, but I said, "I think it's a question everyone asks. At least you found the books to read, and they gave you the latitude to read. In some other household, even reading storybooks would have been contentious. Though I suspect that they would have been happier if you had managed to find your comfort in something more domestically useful or—"

"Found God?" We both laughed. She said, "I thought about finding God but *She* was more fun. And *Treasure Island.*"

"I think so as well," I replied, and touched her arm. She lowered her eyes and sat back in her chair, playing with her bangle. "We used to play Monopoly, and when your uncle Vijay returned from England, he so triumphantly corrected our pronunciation of 'Reading Railroad.' I had had such a lovely vision of a steam train puffing clouds of steam and all the plump, tweedy passengers cozily reading about a gory murder in the penny dreadfuls. And Vijay completely dissipated my elaborate fantasy."

I used to read in any quiet nook I could find in the house, which was not so easy, our house being so much smaller than my paati's ramshackle home. In her house, I chose the roof when it was dry, and the attic in the monsoon season. How many hours I had spent reading in the half-dark attic, sitting on the floor just close enough to the barred windows to benefit from sunlight sieved through banana tree leaves, and just far enough away to elude the scattering rain. And when I came downstairs, my pavadai-chokka would be smeared with dust. "Chi, what have you done? Instead of visiting your paati, you go roll yourself in dirt," my mother would say.

But in her way, I think, she was proud of my bookishness, some small compensation for two unstudious sons, and she knew what it was to want to evade what the company of others imposed. When my father's family arrived, she would throw a pinch of mustard into a pan, and shout from the kitchen, "I'll come, I'll come, I'm just thalchikottifying." By the time the relatives went home, we would have mountains of vettral.

My husband has a cousin sister whose every pallu, handkerchief, shawl, tablecloth, curtain is embroidered by her with countless little flowers and mangos and birds, so her house makes one almost dizzy with the agitation of all her useless intensity flourishing in this wordless way. Indira tended to her plants even as she was dying of cancer, her bare, bald head aggravating her son, who did not want her showing her sickness in front of the house. Indira of the rose bushes, whose father boxed her ears so badly she was partially deaf in one ear before she finished college or acquired a husband. I thought then that Indira advised me as a way of coaxing me into taking her side, into displaying my empathy for her in front of the rest of the family, but it was only her concern that I be told what she had had to laboriously discover for herself. I don't think I wanted to know what she meant. But in whatever room made private by the book in front of my face, I relaxed in a way that was not possible with others, even those I loved, with whom I censored myself by the byzantine rules of family life, social norms, the rule of power and the limits of each imagination. I accepted my husband because with his earnest absorption in his research, he had the sense of other people as strange and mysterious, allowing others at least the freedom not to have to fight against presuppositions of who they were. My father would buy me bright orange half-saris flush with the insistence that this was my favourite colour, because my taste for dark greens and mustards was to his eyes unacceptable in a young girl. To have a husband who could not imagine what colour sari should be my favourite, or for that matter remember which I have claimed as favourite, was and is a kind of luxury. And too, I have my research, whose subject absorbs my concentration when I sit curled behind the mask of dutiful attention at faculty meetings or family gatherings, as once in my younger days, I threaded the lines of Kubla Khan or the exploits of Don Quixote. Lacking the conviction to confect my secret life out of my own longings, I pieced together the adventures of others between, or behind, nods, murmurs and smiles of responsive interest. And my need was not so great, or not often great.

"So what were you looking for, if it wasn't people getting hacked?" said Anjolie. "I know all of the books were yours because you had your name in the front, 'Library of Ambikai.'"

"I think everyone reading a story looks for some of the same things," I said to her. "Signs of other lives, ways of escaping our own lives, if only for an hour or two." And as the hour was almost time for me for the seminar that I was teaching, I turned to other subjects, the normal familial business, and the generalities of life on the campus.

Sometime later in the week, when I found myself in the main library of the university on the trail of a privately published memoir by a Indo-Mauritian trader, I sought out a copy of *Treasure Island* to see how it withstood the passage of time. The story seemed vaguely familiar without my being to recall any particular incident as such, and I wondered if even its familiarity was a projection of my knowing that I had once read it. Other books came with their occasions more clearly—*Northanger Abbey* always had the flavour of the especially sweet rabdi I was eating as I first read it, and *War and Peace* puts me into mind of a hotel in Ooty.

I skimmed through the book, looking as I could through Anjolie's frame of mind, and paused to read more carefully when I came to this passage:

> I snatched a cutlass from the pile, and someone, at the
> same time snatching another, gave me a cut across the
> knuckles which I hardly felt. I dashed out of the door into
> the clear sunlight. Someone was close behind, I knew not
> whom. Right in front, the doctor was pursuing his
> assailant down the hill, and just as my eyes fell upon him,
> beat down his guard, and sent him sprawling on his back,
> with a great slash across his face.

It didn't seem quite violent enough for satisfaction, but I could imagine it gaining in vividity from the richness of her own feelings. So many years ago, Indira had told me that she curled her self into her chest so that what my uncle beat was only the shell in which she resided, that she lived like a seed rattling in a tamarind pod, and only with her hands in the wet soil, with the smell of rose in her nostrils, could she feel her self expand to the surface of her skin, into the palms of her hands. I could envision Anjolie, with her utter inability to bridge the distance between herself and her father's family, her knot of self tightened in self-protection and by their inability to see her as she is, finally loosening into herself and gaining instruction as she could take it, in the attic room whose emptiness, silence, space, half-darkness had attracted me as well.

And there, with book before her, she could escape, but in another sense take fuller possession of those rooms of herself to which she had no other key. It flattered me to think that, without knowing how, I had found a way to bring her out of the rest of her life, and there was something nicely chastening in the fact that this was achieved not by my words of advice, but through things I had once owned.

MINA KUMAR

Water

THE APARTMENT was cold. Venu was wearing a wool sweater over his long-sleeved banian, and long underwear under his cords, but still he was cold. He sat at his desk with a Woolworth's blanket over his legs, trying to read, but the temperature seemed to have dropped to the absolute zero at which his neurons could not fire. He closed the book—a tome on Oracle—and hunched over it, its slick cover against his cheek.

He had no idea what to do. Avinash, Venu's room-mate, had gone home for the holidays, so he could not be deputized to deal with it as he had been before. Avinash knew how to deal with things, and more importantly, knew how to yell at the super. Avinash had gotten their broken toilet seat replaced, although the seat's condition was a matter of indifference to him, simply because he enjoyed screaming obscenities in English, Hindi and Spanish at the super, and the super's wife, who guarded her husband against all intrusions. Venu, on the other hand, could not bear to even speak to the super, whose accent Venu found impenetrable, much less the super's wife, whose English was even worse, and who gave Venu even less opportunity to speak.

Venu wanted the super to make sure the radiator was opened to its maximum. When it first started getting cold, Avinash had used his pliers to open the radiator even more. Then, on warmer days, he had tightened it to reduce the heat in the apartment.

For the hundredth time, Venu got up to look at it. He pushed his chair back and went over to Avinash's bed. He put his cupped palms over the radiator as he would put his hands over the fire of a tambalam. There was only the palest and mildest of heat, like the breath from a baby's mouth. He crouched in front of it, squeezed against Avinash's bed, and tried to move the tap-like thing at its foot. He could barely move it either way. He tried until his palm began to hurt, and then gave up, nursing his hand. There was a little tear where his middle finger met his palm.

He went to sit on his own bed. Avinash's bed was too filthy to be sat on. Venu had the disagreeable feeling that the sheets were encrusted with semen. Avinash, at night, masturbated with no regard for Venu sleeping not five feet away from him.

For that, and other, reasons, Venu was glad he was gone. Many nights, Venu had come back to the room from the library or the Computer Centre and found some giggling girl sitting on Avinash's bed, as Avinash lay sprawled on his pillows. Only with Suganthi had it been different. Venu had come home to the smell of the rasam she had been reheating in the kitchen. Avinash had been sick with the flu.

Finally, Venu picked up the telephone which sat on the bookshelf between the beds. For the third night in a row, Venu tried to call the super, to explain the pressing need for more heat in the apartment, to find out if the heat from the boiler could be increased, and for the third night, the super's wife answered and said, "Whaa? Whaa? Jorge not here. He come see you in the morning," and hung up the phone.

The windows rattled in their frames. Despite the towels Venu had rolled and placed against the window ledge, cold air still rushed out from where the glass met the frames, and where the frames met the wall. It turned his sheets cold. He lay down in bed and wrapped them tightly around his body so that they could absorb what body heat he had.

He had already tried calling the other boys he knew: Raghu, Mani, Ranga. Ranga had told him to buy a space-heater, which Venu was too embarrassed to say that he could not afford. Mani, who was at least less insensitive, told Venu to turn on the oven. Since their rent included utilities, this was a more viable plan of action. Venu had meticulously cleaned the oven with Oven-Off and wiped it with a moistened cloth, before turning it on and leaving the door open. Half an hour later, he found himself nauseated and almost swooning from the oven's emanations. Whatever it was—incomplete combustion, gas leak, too much carbon dioxide—it wasn't healthy, and he'd turned the oven off.

He'd tried drinking Ovaltine. Venu even liked Ovaltine, which his Amma had often given him for tiffin along with Digestive biscuits and seasonal fruit, but he found that two mugs of it formed his natural limit. He'd tried wearing his woollen socks and knit beret, but it was too uncomfortable, and did not make him feel much warmer. He had forced himself to read, using Mani's final suggestion of mind over matter. His mind faltered.

Venu lay in bed, as he had done for most of the last three evenings. During working hours, he went to the Computer Centre on campus, and tried to work. The Computer Centre was air-conditioned, and even more unpleasant than his room, but he had a great deal to do. When he came home, he would cook some rice, and eat, and then find himself incapable of doing anything else. He was not keeping his carefully made schedule for his holidays. He felt unpleasantly indolent. With Avinash and Suganthi gone, he knew no one in the building whose help he could request. He would have even rung up Suganthi's room-mate, but she too was gone for the break.

The first time Lisa had come to his room with Suganthi, she'd told him of all the calamities that had occurred in the building in her three years there. Venu had been disgusted by her manner. She had seated herself on Avinash's bed, without being invited to do so, and ignoring the empty chair beside Suganthi, despite the fact that Venu was standing so that she could sit there. Lisa had sat cross-legged on the bed, her dirty blonde hair hanging limply down her face, and told them about the rape that occurred during Spring Break her first year, the rat epidemic of another year, the time the water had been shut off for two days.

Suganthi had laughed. "Lisa, we're used to it, coming from India. My family gets its water from a pump in the front yard."

Venu had been surprised that she said this. He felt it incumbent upon himself to announce that American music videos were now available on Indian television and that Japanese car manufacturers were eager to sell in the vast Indian market. In any case, Venu's family had their water coming into the apartment, though they hadn't the means to tap into the main line or dig their own well.

Lisa had said that the building had boiler problems every year. The boiler had broken down completely the previous winter. She had tried everything from wearing her parka to bed to huddling around a lamp with a 200 W bulb and no lampshade. "A 90's fireplace," Lisa had said, shaking her head. In the end, she'd filled up her bathtub with boiling hot water. It had warmed the room and helped her asthma, too. She'd tried to form a group of students to conduct a sit-in protest in the administrative building but the boiler had been fixed before they managed to organize themselves. Venu had expected her to be some species of Marxist, like the collegiate protesters he knew in India, but she had said she was not interested in ideology because that was bullshit, and she was more into spirituality. "I think I'm into Buddhism," Lisa had said, flicking her hair out of her eyes. "Are there a lot of Buddhists in India?" Venu had shaken his head, then caught Suganthi smiling at him sardonically.

Now she was with her family for the holidays. She had relatives in New Jersey, an aunt who ran a centre for immigrant women out of the basement of her house, and an uncle who was a paraplegic.

Venu swallowed, and pulled the sheets more tightly around him. He missed Suganthi, he missed her soothing manner, and her rasam. Something really karam would warm him. He thought of Suganthi's fiery sambars, and the long-finished gonkura chutney she had given him. His mouth became wet, and he swallowed again. Suganthi used garlic and onions liberally, unlike his own mother, who was afraid that they would excite his passions. The first time Venu had eaten Suganthi's cooking, the time Avinash was sick, she had smiled to see Venu's appetite, and asked if the food was OK. Except she'd said "sor," not "saatham." Venu had flinched, and then tried to disguise it as a shudder from the cold.

Venu turned towards the window. Snow was falling heavily. It looked like a solarized picture of a television after programming hours were over. The wind whined like a pey. He hugged his chest. What was he supposed to do? He felt as if he would collapse if he didn't do something. He thought about eating, even though his belly was already taut from his dinner and the tea. Finally, he got up and turned the light on in the kitchen, a roach scurrying behind the fridge. The kitchen was well-stocked with salves for sudden desires for karam: store-bought coriander chutney for sandwiches or samosas; urgas for thayir saatham; Mohan's Madras Curry Powder to mix into ketchup or Ramen noodles; long dried red chillies for curries; red pepper flakes for Chinese delivery or pizza. He opened the fridge and took up the chutney, but finally put it back and went back into bed.

He rewrapped himself in his sheets, wiggling his toes. Under the sheets and blankets, under his clothes, he was still shivering. He lay with his hands under his buttocks, but they still did not warm.

If Mani or Raghu or even Ranga had invited him to stay with them, he would have gladly gone, but they did not. In any case, they were at the movie theatre watching some movie about big-breasted go-go dancers competing for the go-go grand prize. Mani had asked Venu, pro forma, to join them, but Venu neither wanted to spend the money nor feel obliged to ogle the women. What Venu wanted was to stay home and read his Oracle book.

And even the guilty, slothful pleasure of lying in bed, doing nothing, was not possible when his body was so cold and itchy from layers of clothing. Venu was not used to having his arms covered day in and day out, and he felt as if his skin was being sealed up with gum. He absolutely could not wear socks in the apartment, even if it would make him a little bit warmer.

Finally, the light still on, Venu fell asleep, but after an hour he awoke. He went for a piss, then came back, and stood in front of the windows. It was still snowing. The windows shook so much that they seemed about to shatter. The towels had fallen to the ground. Venu bent down and picked them up. They were damp and cold, with little flakes of snow along the folds. He flung them across the room, and rubbed his hands together.

He couldn't bear it any more. He couldn't bear the discomfort, the irritation, the boredom of not having concentration enough to read. He paced in what little room there was in the apartment. between the desks and the beds. He wanted heat. He thought of taking a hot shower but he knew it would only make him feel worse when he came back into the cold. But there seened to be no other way. He charged into the bathroom and opened the bathtub's hot water tap.

He sat on the rim of the tub and waited. It took nearly five minutes for the water to turn hot. He peeled off his clothes, got in the tub and yanked the shower curtain closed. Standing under the showerhead, he let the water fall hot and hard against his neck, and down his back and chest, then tipped his head back to wet his face. He rubbed his cake of soap lazily over his chest, careful to avoid his punal. He had once considered bathing a chore, but the water pressure was so strong that he felt as if the spray was massaging his neck, more powerfully, more sensually, than hands rubbing in oil. He lathered under his armpits. The hot water tap was opened to its maximum, and steam rose in puffs over the shower curtain rod. Venu felt his body slowly livening up, as if his pores were opening one by one. He bent down and scrubbed his legs with soap, up his thighs, then onto his belly. He lathered his arms, and his chest. He felt like a potato whose dirty skin comes loose in hot water, revealing its fair, clean body. He returned the soap to its box on the plastic rack Avinash had nailed to the wall. Most of the things on the rack belonged to Avinash—Venu still did not appreciate the purpose of conditioner nor did he care for bubble bath. Avinash, however, liked to take baths for hours, reading *Sports Illustrated,* and no doubt masturbating. Next to the Mr. Bubbles bubble bath was the plug Avinash had bought at Woolworth's, their tub not having had one when they moved in.

Venu stepped out of the tub, the water still running. He wrapped a towel around his waist, then held the shower curtains apart and watched the steaming hot water rushing down. It sluiced down the drain, through the perforated metal piece. Venu took the plug and pressed it into place. He went into the other room to put on a fresh, soft banian and tie on a veshti. It was still very cold, so he took a blanket and his book and returned to the bathroom, leaving the door open. He spread the blanket over the laundry basket, sat on top of the clothes, and began to read where he left off.

The hot water poured on and on. It was like being next to a waterfall. For the first time in days, Venu felt happy. It reminded him of going to the waterfall in Mysore as a child, when his father was still alive. He read his book, careful to note how close the water was reaching to the brim. When the tub was full, he turned off the tap, and decided to go back to sleep. He marked his place in the book with a leaf of paper, and set it on the desk. He went to bed, pulling the sheets over him. The room felt a little warmer, the air rich and heavy. He drifted off to sleep.

It was the best sleep he had had in days. He did not awake once in the middle of the night. It was noon before he finally sat up. Sunlight streaked across his face, his thighs. He combed his hair with his fingers, thinking. It was Saturday, and the Computer Centre was closed. Usually on Saturdays, it was open but closed early, and afterwards, he went to the Indian grocery to buy food or he visited with Mani. Mani's American room-mate was learning the veena and he had a vast collection of Carnatic CD's. On Sundays, Venu usually went for a long walk in the park, and read the newspaper. It was too cold for the park, and he did not want to call Mani. He decided to make some tea and read the chapters of the Oracle book he had planned to finish by now.

He went into the bathroom to wash his face and brush his teeth. The water still in the tub was a surprise to him, and he held the shower curtain open gingerly, examining it. He had forgotten to scrub the tub before he filled it, and he could see lines of scum through the water. He cupped a palmful. It was cold and smelled stale. He threw it back in. It was not dirty water, exactly, but not clean either. He had no idea what to do with it. It was no longer doing anything to warm the room, but could he just pull the plug and send it down the drain?

He decided to leave it for now. He brushed his teeth and washed his face and shaved. Then he went to the radiator. The heat it emitted seemed even slighter. Venu gave an exasperated sigh. It was pointless to call the super. He would go down there himself. He dressed again in his dark brown sweater, long underwear and cords, and went to the basement, where the super had his apartment next to the laundry room. He knocked on the door.

First he knocked politely, but then he slammed his fist against the door. His knuckles hurt, but there was no answer, no response from behind the door. He put his ear against it to see if he could hear anything. Then he bent down to see if there was any light coming out from underneath. He heard footsteps coming into the laundry room, so he straightened up and went back to his room.

Once inside his room, he rubbed his knuckles against his cheek, leaning against the door. It was beginning to snow again. Maybe if he got heavy curtains to replace the blinds, it would be better. But how much would curtains cost? He made some tea and toast, and ate them reading his book. Once or twice in the day, he went and looked at the tub full of water.

As the day wore on, he became more and more conscious of the wasted water, more and more conscious of its weight, the way he would slowly notice that it had been hours, and sometimes even days, since his mother had spoken more than a few words to him. Since his father had died, his mother and his aunt never uttered so much as a word of reproach, but when they were worried by something he had done, their silence would grow deeper and thicker, like roots growing into the soil. "Venu, yen-ma, when you know that your Amma has heart-strain...," Bhama Mami would say quietly at his most serious infractions. Though they never used their silence to make him do anything, it was their only response when he did something that they thought was hurtful for him: ate chicken, or visited a girl classmate, or kept the light on reading storybooks late into the night, or took a bath in the evening after playing cricket. As for action, they did for themselves. His mother rose at five to take her bath with the first water on days when the water came and filled the electric cistern so he would have hot water for his bath, then Bhama Mami would fill the stainless steel buckets with water she would later boil for kitchen use, then filling the plastic buckets for toilet and cleaning uses, and bathe herself. Venu usually only went in just as the water began to die out.

When his other aunt, Malathi, came to visit, she spitefully kept the generator on for hours, and spilled buckets of water, and spoilt the flour by getting water into it. She had once even managed to leave the almari with the jewellery in it unlocked while the servant was there, except that the servant merely closed it and went on sweeping.

And like Malathi, who lived in Singapore, Venu was acquiring extravagant habits. He stirred the water with his fingertip. He could boil it, and use it to wash the dishes at least. But their tub was old and deep, and it held at least a hundred and seventy-five litres of water. They had a carpet in the room, so he couldn't use it for washing the floors.

Venu sat down on the laundry basket full of clothes, not even bothering to put a blanket on top. His shoulders and arms and buttocks were prickled with goosebumps. He curled his body over his knees, holding his toes in his hands. They were cold and cracked, veins of dryness reaching up from the callouses. He sat there in the bathroom, at first trying to think about what do with the water, and his thoughts fell more haphazardly, to the way drinking water from a plastic cup smelled to him like the water in the plastic buckets in the bathroom, watching his father standing on the balcony and shaving as his mother washed the tulsi, the way Suganthi would turn the tap off when Lisa was scrubbing the heel of a pot, receiving his first receipt here and fondling the thickness of the paper, the cricket bat he had cracked by swatting it against the front gate, the way his mother had hugged him to her in the hospital when it was clear his father would die, the way neither his mother nor his aunt had expressed anything but joy that he had received his scholarship though they worried even when he went out to buy matches, the smell of the hair oil Avinash had teased him out of using, the warmth of lying in his bed every Saturday afternoon reading the comic books he had bought in the morning, the crows that would come to the balcony and eat the rice they had left for the sparrows. Already the memories were brightening and shrinking, coins in an album. He could feel the shape of his life changing beneath his feet. He rested his cheek on his knees.

At some point he fell asleep, and then he awoke to the darkened bathroom, teeth chattering, to see the mirror glinting in the light of the street lamps outside. He looked down, eyes gluey with sleep. The arm of a sweatshirt of Avinash's curled over the edge of the laundry basket and onto the floor. Venu pulled it out and spread it on the tile floor, folding it over his feet. Then he put his face against his knees and fell asleep again. He dreamt of being home, and pouring buckets and buckets of water into a septic tank full of faeces.

He awoke when Avinash slapped the side of his head. "What the hell are you doing?" Avinash asked, his thick eyebrows furrowed. "Why the hell are you sleeping in the laundry basket?" It was still dark outside. Venu opened his eyes. He couldn't tell if it was Sunday morning or evening, or why Avinash was back. The bathroom door was open, and through the shock of light, Venu could see a frizzy-haired girl sitting on his bed.

"What the fuck is this?" said Avinash, peering into the bathtub. He rolled up the sleeve of his sweater, reached in, and pulled the plug.

AMIT CHAUDHURI

The Old Masters

HE GLANCED at his watch and made an attempt to finish the tea in his cup; he was waiting for a call, and it was his second cup of tea. Five minutes later, the phone began to ring.

'Pramathesh?' said the voice at the other end; and he could tell, from its slight note of insouciance and boredom, that it was Ranjit.

'I was waiting for your call, old man,' he said, trying to muffle his irritation with his usual show of joviality. 'You were supposed to call half an hour ago.' He didn't know why he even bothered to mention this, since Ranjit, who was never known to acknowledge he was late, would take this to be an unnecessarily pedantic remark, a remark that pointed to the actual, if generally concealed, gulf that distinguished their temperaments.

'Trying to send the boy off to school... didn't want to go this morning,' he muttered. 'That boy'll cost me my job one of these days.'

'Come, come, don't blame it on poor Mithu. He has enough

troubles being an innocent bystander in your life. Are we ready?'

'Of course I'm ready! Should we say ten minutes?' As an after-thought, a change of register: 'Sorry I didn't call earlier.'

You can't choose your colleagues in the office; he hadn't grasped the significance of this until a few months ago. And to pretend you were friends—that, too, was a fiction you couldn't bring yourself wholly to believe in, but couldn't entirely dispense with either; you did 'things' together, sometimes outside office hours, you visited each other's house—he'd been to Ranjit's place in New Alipore only day before yesterday—got to know each other's wife and children, the kind of food the wife, affectionately referred to as the 'grihini', cooked, and, yet, you made a pact to keep all that was true and most important about yourself from the colleague; in case the desirable boundary between private life and secret nightmare and employment ceased to exist. Meanwhile, your real friends, those mythological beings, who by now had embarked on lives and careers of their own, fell obligingly by the wayside, they became things you put inside a closet and meant to recover, some day, in the future. In other words, you were alone, with your family, and your destiny.

Pramathesh Majumdar had joined the company three years ago, soon after coming back from England in 1964 as a Chartered Accountant. A brief honeymoon period with office life and work in Calcutta ensued, which also saw this makeshift arrangement, this friendship, with Ranjit Biswas come into being. Ranjit had never been abroad; he'd been born and brought up in Calcutta. He had the ease and the unquestioning expectancy of routine repeating itself, and of things continuing to fit, that belong to one who has never been removed from his original habitat.

Pramathesh belonged nowhere; he came, originally, from East Bengal; his sights were probably set somewhere higher. Although Ranjit Biswas was still, strictly speaking, a colleague, both knew, though this wasn't articulated, that Pramathesh, in his unassuming way, was preparing himself for the race people called 'professional life', while Ranjit, with his impatience with keeping appointments, was perhaps going to stay in the same place for some time, feeling, now and then, bitter, without being unduly bothered to do anything about it. It was the strength of Pramathesh's British degree that gave him a head start, of course, but it was also something else, a meticulousness which might be called foresight. In fact, Pramathesh had been transferred to the Delhi office in June this year, and since the Delhi office was now the head office, this move had been interpreted as a promotion.

Today's mission was the outcome of a chance remark made the day before yesterday. He'd been sitting at Ranjit's place after dinner, contemplating returning to the guest house; he said, stretching his arms, 'Well, I'm returning to Delhi next week. Have to get down to some shopping.' 'Like what, Pramathesh da?' asked Ranjit's wife, Malini, as she was putting away the dishes. 'The usual things, I suppose,' said Pramathesh, who looked younger than his thirty nine years. 'Go to Gariahat, buy a few saris; decorations; take some gandharaj lime—my son loves those...' In his heart of hearts, he missed Calcutta; Delhi seemed small and transitory and provincial in comparison. 'How did the project with the boss go this time?' asked Ranjit, lighting a cigarette (his wife called him a 'chain smoker') and leaning against the wicker chair in the verandah. There was curiosity in his voice, and a hint of competitiveness. 'Oh all right,' said Pramathesh, sounding non-committal, but actually engrossed in the mental picture of Lahiri as it hovered before him, a quiet, balding man with fair, tissue-paper-like skin who wore glasses with thick lenses and looked as if nothing had changed noticeably since the years before Independence. He could hear his voice and his cough. 'You know, generous and friendly when he's in a good mood, and slightly unfathomable when he's not.' Ranjit nodded, and took a fresh puff on his cigarette. 'Are you thinking of taking back a two kg rui from the fish market?' said Malini from the semi-lit dining room, her voice holding back laughter. 'I saw you eating today, and thought, "He doesn't get fish there."' 'Yes, that's right,' said Pramathesh, 'I'll just give it to the air-hostess and tell her to hang on to it until we land.' 'A lot of people take back mishti doi,' said Ranjit. He began to laugh in his unobtrusively nasty, dry manner, which meant that he was going to reveal something that had given him pleasure at someone else's expense. 'I saw a man standing in line for security at the airport with a huge bhaad of doi, and the next time I saw him the bhaad had fallen to ground and shattered, the yoghurt lay on the floor in a tragic mess: the poor man, he looked lost and heartbroken! I don't think we'll see him in Calcutta in a hurry!' After a few moments, Pramathesh said quietly, 'I was thinking of taking back a picture... something nice—to hang up in the new flat.' 'A picture?'

There were still hardly any art galleries in Calcutta. And the idea of buying a painting—and not a print—was still an unusual one. But, recently, at a cocktail party in a superior's bungalow in Delhi, Pramathesh's wife had noticed an original Nandalal Bose. Not that she'd known it was an original; but someone told her it was. Returning to their own flat, she'd said it might be a good idea to buy a decent painting for their drawing room; it would be their first stab at creating a status that would be in accordance with Pramathesh's professional life. Now, Ranjit racked his brains and said, 'Well, I know where Gopal Ghosh lives: we could go there.' Of course, owning a Gopal Ghosh may not be owning a Picasso; but his paintings were held in high regard. Just as Pramathesh's career as a Chartered Accountant and an employee was at the fledgling stage, so was the Indian art world, with its ambivalences and lack of self-belief. Paradoxically, it was those who might be accused of not understanding art who would nourish it, unknowingly, through this delicate moment, setting up a concomitance between its life and theirs. It was as if their lives were destined, in some sense, to be connected and to grow together, though this must not be seen to be so.

So the two men decided to meet in front of the office itself in Chowringhee, at a quarter past ten on Saturday, before the seven-storeyed building. An old, moustached watchman who had nothing much to occupy him hovered in the background while Pramathesh waited for Ranjit to arrive. When he did, he instructed his driver to remain parked where he was. From there, they went in Ranjit's white Ambassador, the driver in front wordless, down a main artery, which was fairly deserted on a Saturday, towards one of the by-lanes in an area quite far from both New Alipore and the company guest house; Pramathesh, in fact, didn't know what it was called. Here, they came to a ground floor flat in an old two-storeyed house in a narrow lane facing, and flanked by, other houses not unlike itself. They were not sure if they should just walk in, but when they did, finding the door open, they found no one inside; only the ceiling fan hung immobile above them.

The painter, emerging into the living room a few minutes later to discover them, didn't seem to mind their intrusion. He was wearing a dhuti and a shabby jacket himself, and looked abstracted; he glanced at the two men in their pressed shirt-sleeves, trousers, and sandals, and appeared to make a shrewd appraisal of why they were here and who they might be. 'Was it you who just came up in the car?' he asked, to which Pramathesh said, a little hesitantly, 'Yes.' He finally sold Pramathesh two of his paintings very matter-of-factly, bringing them from a room inside, one showing a pale, white forest, in which the trees were crested with white blossoms, with probably a peasant woman walking in it, and the other of a group of figures, possibly pilgrims, walking dimly past a mountainside. One might have missed their appeal; indeed, Pramathesh had to summon up something forgotten inside him, something from his early youth, in order to respond to them. It was not a faculty he had to use often, or of late; and he wasn't altogether sure of his judgement. At any rate, without quite knowing why, he bought the two paintings for one hundred and fifty rupees each.

Two days later, Pramathesh left Calcutta. As had been apparent, he continued, as the next decade unfolded, to do substantially better than Ranjit Biswas. His rise even surprised himself. Ranjit remained more or less stationary, with the prospect of a small promotion in the next five years; while Pramathesh was transferred to Bombay, and made General Manager at the Bombay branch. The last old master he bought was a Jamini Roy, in 1969, again on a visit to Calcutta in the winter. By then, Calcutta was in decline; the branch was experiencing a series of lock-outs, and Ranjit was sounding more and more beleaguered and nonplussed, as if he'd just found out that he was fighting the battle alone. 'It's difficult to be in control any more, bhai. They,' he meant the workers, 'are the bosses now; we run behind them,' he said, a little self-conscious in his defensiveness, and partly because Pramathesh was now, technically, no longer a colleague; the old banter had a slight fakeness about it. Jamini Roy was already an old man, and, during this visit, Pramathesh went to the painter's house with Amita, his wife, small and bright in a printed silk sari, about to assume life in Bombay; the old man, in a vest and dhuti, tottered out, and signed the paintings on the floor. When asked innocently by Amita, 'What time of the day do you paint?' he responded like any cantankerous old man, 'How can I answer that? Can I tell you when I eat, or drink, or sleep?' Upside down on the floor before them lay the paintings, the ideal figures with over-large eyes that did not see, the repetitive shapes in repose.

It's not as if Pramathesh and Amita Majumdar spent too much time thinking about these paintings; Bombay didn't give one much time to think. They moved from drawing room to drawing room as the couple themselves moved about in Bombay, from Worli to Kemp's Corner to Malabar Hill. And it wasn't as if they were insensitive to art; nor were they pretentiously artistic; they were content to display them, respectfully, on the walls. Of course, they—the paintings—did coincide with that part of the couple that was defined by their natural ambition, by Pramathesh's career and his concern for the future, but in an odd way, so that the paintings somewhat transcended, or ignored, these vivid concerns. They were probably an unexplored part of their lives. Meanwhile, Jamini Roy, who'd already seemed so old, died peacefully in 1972. Gopal Ghosh died in penury and neglect about five years later, his last days an alcoholic stupor, often drinking himself to sleep on the pavement, and being carried home by passers-by.

On subsequent visits to Calcutta (and they did need to make visits, because they had relatives here, and occasionally there were weddings), Pramathesh and his wife were spared the embarrassment of having to meet the Biswases too frequently, because Ranjit had lost his job and joined a Marwari company that made ceiling and table fans, where he seemed reasonably happy, and able to conceal from himself the fact that here, too, the prospects for advancement were of a limited nature. But he had a better position than before; and, since Pramathesh was appointed to the Board in 1977, it was just as well they didn't meet except in the lobby of the Calcutta Club by accident, or at Lake Market, where they came upon each other with surprised exclamations and hurriedly exchanged pleasantries before saying goodbye. Former colleagues are happy to meet and depart from each other like ghosts, in an evanescent zone of their own making that lies somewhere between their working life, leisure time, memory, and the future. Nothing is final about these meetings until they retire, and they can review the shape of their achievements. Even then, their children, who may have entirely forgotten each other, have the potential to carry on their fathers' rivalries and friendships without knowing it, in their parents' drifting, speculative daydreams. Anyway, Ranjit leaving his job and disappearing in another direction saved Pramathesh the minor embarrassment of having to be his superior, and preside over his career.

The main surprise in Pramathesh's life came from his son, who took up the violin and Western classical music when he was a teenager in a serious way. What had begun as an eccentric but admirable pursuit after school hours became something more than that. One day, the boy came back from school and said, 'Baba, I want to study the violin.' Pramathesh was too disarmed to raise an objection just then; and, as he remained unable to come up with one after two, then three, years, he saw, fondly but with a lurking feeling of helplessness, that his son would level out what he had striven for, that all the sense of certainty and dull, precious predictability and self-sufficiency he had naively built up would now—he was almost grateful for it—become, whether his son succeeded or not (because success in the arts counts for so little) less quantifiable, like a new beginning. His son and grandchildren would lead a life quite different from what he'd thought they would. He sent his son to study the violin in London, and this almost rendered him bankrupt, though his 'almost bankrupt' was still substantially better off than most of his countrymen. He and Amita moved, after his retirement in the mid-Eighties, to a spacious apartment in West Bandra which he had bought twelve years ago for two lakh rupees; they lived here alone, with a servant, going out together now and then to walk in the lane, while their son, finally, settled in the US and married there, making several abortive attempts to inaugurate a career as a musician. The paintings went with them to Bandra, and gazed upon Pramathesh's life without understanding its trajectory, but forgiving it nevertheless by not giving it too much importance. Now and then he gazed back at the paintings, considering what, or who, had given birth to that procession of figures by the mountainside, or that pale forest; those shadowy colours pointed to something he was still content, in his deliberate withdrawal from the imagination, not to understand. Jamini Roy, however, stayed in the drawing room, immutable; and Gopal Ghosh, who had been forgotten by the art world and then lately recovered and re-estimated, was like an enigma that had glancingly touched Pramathesh's working and his private life, near and utterly distant. The world that had produced that curious art, those daubs of green and bold lines, which one never knew, in the end, what to think of, had long ceased to exist; he had made an inroad towards it, by chance, for some other reason, and touched it without ever entering it anything but superficially. History, as if to compensate for that passing, and in a belated consciousness of its own importance, had added to the paintings a value that neither Pramathesh nor the painters would have at first dreamt of; while taking away from him, gradually, his working life, his youth, and the bustling innocence of his adult certainties.

AMIT CHAUDHURI

Prelude to an Autobiography

I FELT the urge to write this after I began to read Shobha De's memoirs. If she can write her memoir, I thought, so can I. For who would have thought, Shobha De least of all, that one day she would write her life-story for other people to read? She had been an ordinary, if beautiful, girl, who got recruited (as she says) from a middle-class home into modelling, never particularly interested in studies (I was the same at her age), and then, through accident and ambition, got married into one of Bombay's richest families, started her own magazine and began writing her own gossip column, got divorced, reinvented herself as a writer of middles for Bombay newspapers, married again, became India's first successful pulp novelist, and now has written her memoirs. Through what a strange chain of events people arrive at the world of writing—and Shobha De's transformation has been one of the most unexpected in my lifetime. It shows me the endless possibilities of the society we have lived in. And I ask myself the question: if she can be a writer, and inscribe her thoughts and impressions in language, why not I?

There's the question, of course, of who would want to read my memoirs, or whatever it is I'm setting out to write—because I'm not altogether sure what it is. But (although I've never seen myself as a writer before) these are questions, I'm certain, that preoccupy (inasmuch as I can enter the mind of a writer) all who write (it's an area I know little about). And it consoles me to think that at one time every writer must have done what I'm doing now, starting out, and not knowing where it was leading to. It's not a feeling you can communicate to someone who's never tried it. Some people, I'm sure, end up taking this route by intention and dedication, after years of preparation—my daughter has a friend who, at thirteen, is already writing lovely poems that have been published in *Femina* and her school magazine; I'm sure she'll be a fine writer one day, and she looks set for that course. Others, like myself, and probably Shobha De, arrive at that route by chance (although Shobha De very differently from me), and it's from her that I take a kind of courage, that she should have ended up a writer, although it makes me smile even as I say it.

Yet I'm not quite sure of my English, though it's the only language I have. My knowledge of the Indian languages is passing; I can speak a smattering of a few, but not read or write any one of them with authority. I was born in Patna, of a Gujarati mother and a father who is a deracinated Andhra Brahmin; my link to any Indian language became, thus, self-evidently tenuous. I'm not sure who'd be interested in any of this, though; why should anyone want to know why I write in English, or who my parents were, or how they came to be my parents? But I take heart from small things, besides the uncontrollable urge to get on with the job at hand, an urge that I don't quite understand; 'small things' like the fact that a new writer comes into being almost every day. This is terrifying, but it also gives me (and, I'm sure, many others like me) the impetus to take the first step. I don't necessarily admire all the writers around me, but sometimes it is good to have their presences about (many of them will not be heard of again) as I start out on this venture.

My husband came in a little earlier from the office yesterday than he usually does, energetic but starved, and he caught me sitting alone, looking out at the sea. 'What are you doing?' he asked quizzically; and I started and I think I looked guilty. I knew we had a party to go to in the evening. How could I tell him that I was trying to do something I became ashamed of the moment he entered, that I was trying to frame a sentence?

I went to a Christian school, and learnt to speak the words of the Lord's prayer before I knew what they were. This was in the hot hall of my convent in Patna, with a few hundred other girls, only a few of whose names I remember. I mumbled the words without knowing what they were, and never have found out; but I spoke them reverentially, and grew up believing in God. Whenever I thought of a Supreme Deity, which was not often, but not altogether infrequently either, it was God I thought of, rather than 'parameshwar' or 'ishwar'. But I have never been inside a church, except as a tourist in Goa.

My father's beliefs were contradictory; that is, his beliefs about religion. His beliefs were to do with human beings, the future of the country, and, most important, the upbringing of children. Children must be given love and pride of place, but career must be given priority, too, for the opportunities it will provide, eventually, one's children. God he hardly mentioned at all, except during the crises in his career, when he would mention him philosophically rather than religiously, saying, for instance, 'Well, no one can change what God has already determined.' When I write these words about him, I feel I'm not only describing my father but a general figure, someone whom many other people will recognise in their father. Mothers and fathers belong half to fiction, anyway; it's not as if you're only their biological offspring; they too have reinvented themselves as parents to give you, while you live, the fiction of themselves.

Whom does one write for? At least one of the answers will have to be—'David Davidar'. When I do put my thoughts in order, when I do finally set out on this project, it's him I shall be thinking of. Because he gives me, and others like me, a valid reason. It gives us hope that someone will rescue our manuscripts, our thoughts put down and carefully typed on paper, from oblivion and eternity. Because I am sure that he doesn't—I don't know him, but I have composed him, as an individual with motives and conceptions and almost no prejudices, willy-nilly, piecemeal from what I've read from twenty or thirty articles about writing and publishing over the last eight or nine years—I'm sure he doesn't consign anything to the dustbin until he's given it a proper chance. And Lord knows, he must have quite a few manuscripts upon his table. Not all of them are from famous people. When he came into our lives about ten or eleven years ago (I can't remember exactly when), it was as if he wasn't quite real—we might have dreamed him up. It was as if he'd come from nowhere. But apparently he actually comes from the South; or at least he looks like a South Indian (I've seen him on television). One day—not too far from now, I hope—my manuscript will be waiting at his table.

Where to begin? As I've said to you, the only language I have is English. I remember learning longhand in kindergarten, rows of letters, first a series of a's, then b's, and so on.

I'm uncomfortable beginning at the beginning. It's not because I'm clever, but because it's a difficult thing, writing. And I haven't had any past experience. I used to write poems, of course, when I was quite young; they were passionate and formless but somehow arranged themselves into short and long lines and stanzas without me having to do much about it. Later, they stopped altogether. I suppose it was because I became not unattractive and, after an awkward puberty, when I wasn't sure of myself, acquired a circle of friends and a 'social life'. You will wonder at the inverted commas, but, in the Seventies, so much of what we did was in inverted commas: 'sex', 'love', 'going all the way'; we all talked about it, but half of it was conversation and fantasy, we didn't go 'all the way.'

I think the early years in Patna, though my memories of them are few, and often random and disconnected, must be the reason why I've never felt I belong here—to Bombay—although this is where I grew up. Yet I never think of myself as a person who 'comes from Bombay'; it's the place I've lived in much of my life. Where do I come from, then? I don't have to go to Gujarat to visit my Gujarati relatives; many of them live here, on Peddar Road. My nani, my mother's mother, died in a third-floor flat in a building at the turning of Peddar Road and Gamadia Road.

You ask me if I feel more South Indian or Gujarati—I don't know. I know a few Telegu words, but my father didn't speak very much in Telegu at home. The language my parents spoke to each other in was English. I grew up in a fifth-floor apartment on

Nepean Sea Road, very near where the small fly-over was built in the Seventies. How many walks my friends, especially Kamini, who lived in the same building, and I took across that fly-over!

Kamini and I too spoke to each other in English, although her parents were from the Andhra as well; but it never occurred to us to experiment with Telegu in our conversation. I don't think we even had a clear idea that we were South Indians, I at least in part; the solidarity we felt had to do with the fact that we went to the same school. The English we spoke in, I now realize, was garnished with Hindi words for effect; it all sounded very clever-clever: 'Didn't do too well in my chemistry paper. Chalta hai, yaar!' This was our esperanto, and we never thought to think it anything but English; it wouldn't have done to speak in any other kind of English. The girls who spoke in 'perfect' English were slightly ridiculous, and were supposed to be 'goody-goody.'

That's exactly the esperanto that Shobha De (then Rajadhyaksha) and her colleagues began to write in *Stardust* in the Seventies. There was something slightly impolite about that language, wasn't there?—all right for schoolgirls to speak in, but to *write* in...?

Although so many people write these days (so many, it's difficult to imagine), you feel the world you know, the India you know, is still to be written about. Is this merely solipsistic? Shobha (I hope she won't mind me using her first name) has scratched the tip of the iceberg, though; I now feel that her life is also in some way mine—I don't mean the celebrity; though even celebrity emerges from that book, *Selective Memory* (what an apposite, an inevitable name!), as a kind of character, a desirable freak that some people got to know in Bombay at that time, rather than as destiny. Even the portfolio of photographs, the author now with

Amitabh Bachchan, or Indira Gandhi, or Nari Hira, looks slightly doctored, as if all the photos of Shobha De had been taken on the same day, for she is the same—perpetually young, her carved face immutable—in all of them, while the others—Nari Hira, Amitabh Bachchan—are fraught with contingency, they look like tres- passers. I've seen the tricks that are possible these days; that's why John F Kennedy looks like an intruder, alone and slightly nervous, when he's made to shake hands in *Forrest Gump* with Tom Hanks without being certain he's in the movie.

But that's not what I mean when I say that Shobha De's life is in some way mine. It's not the celebrity; it's the detritus that we all know but no one speaks of, the banal, briefly glittering sequence of events, where the heart beats underneath. That is what I'm concerned with; because that is when I feel myself in the silence, on the edge of the words, not yet a writer (just as she is not yet a writer) but listening to what we in the upper middle class in Bombay frivolously call 'life'. Because, however much we insist, we will never quite be writers; literature is not where we start from. All those years, going to the matinee, borrowing books from the British Council, thinking you might be acquiring a boyfriend—literature was not what proscribed or described those episodes. Of course, we read books (I think Shobha did as well), and I even studied English literature; but that was studying other people's lives, authors and characters. Where our hearts beat, that was secret, or disappointing, or satisfying, or trivial, too trivial for it to become words or a story. Really, our lives were glamorous and happy but too trivial. And it is there that I must begin, that is why all of us writers who have still not written a word are impatient to disturb the silence.

S U K E T U   M E H T A

Sexual History
of an Accountant

WHAT DO I put of myself in my work? asked the accountant. Half
of me, he responded. The juggling of figures, the assignation of
debit and credit, the placing of the tangible and the intangible into
categories and the reconciliation at the end—these are the satis-
factions of my craft. Those numbers, whether they are in ledgers
or on computer screens, represent things: cars, loaves of bread,
taxi drivers' time, industrial machinery, real estate. But to me the
world is simplified, it is contained in digits. I could estimate the
value of anything except emotion. For who knows better than an
accountant that love is priceless? Can you imagine taking a deduc-
tion on love, depreciating its book value? So: this has been the
other half of my life, which is concerned with finding love. True
Love.

After my workday is finished, at 6:30 each evening, I leave the
office and go through the taverns and eateries of the city in which
I live, searching for True Love. I have met numbers of women.

They are attracted to the stability of my profession. I dine with them; I interview them closely, trying to ascertain whether she is the One who can provide me with True Love. Sometimes I need to meet her more than once. Sometimes I have terminated the interview midway through dinner; I tell the woman clearly, "I'm sorry. I'm searching for True Love and I don't think you're the One." They are surprised, of course, occasionally hurt and angry, but they appreciate my frankness and thereupon evince a keen interest in my search, asking me all kinds of questions about it. A good many of them generously offer to set me up with their friends or relatives that they think have what I'm looking for, and I always accept.

Might I think that I am promiscuous? the accountant asked. No, he answered, because in all these years of my quest I have only completed sexual intercourse with four of these women. These four had reached an advanced stage in the process, and any of them could have been the One. Many others, lonely or just propelled by intelligent desire, would have been happy to share my bed without expectation of longevity in our relationship. But of course, that would have been out of the question. Let me, though, think about the women that I investigated sexually.

The first was a Cuban. She came at an early stage in my life, when I had not formulated the parameters of my quest fully. Hence, although I knew vaguely that I was looking for the special person, I was not so deliberate about it. The Cuban girl—Elena— cost me my virginity. I lost substantial sums of money on her. It is not that she was a professional woman or anything, it is just that she came from a deprived background and needed money spent on her. I was considerably more junior in the firm than I am now, and I had not much money, but what I had I used to buy her meals, entertainment, apparel, cosmetics, and travel. However, I was emotionally and physically rewarded. My time with her was binary, spent in one of two mental states: exhilaration or misery.

Finally we parted company because she saw something sinful in our physical relationship. She had lately rediscovered her Catholicism. I believe I might have accepted an offer of marriage had she made a proposal. Does that mean she was the One? Looking back on it, I am convinced not. I was young.

The second was, one might put it figuratively, from my tribe. She had grown up not far from me, in the suburb. Although I journeyed outward from there, we kept in touch occasionally and when I met her in the city, I was struck by a theretofore unknown chord of nostalgia, or at least of familiarity. We spoke of the few entertainment emporia and storehouses of goods that we had known when we were young; they had almost all closed by now, she informed me. The people we knew, who were not many to begin with, had moved away or grown old beyond recognition. I had never gone back after University; she had, a few times, to create memories. But now she was living in the city, working in a laboratory. She had no roommate and the decor of her apartment reflected that; all three rooms were preternaturally neat since she had the space to store everything in its proper place. Her stereo system was large, and in the living room.

She was obviously pleased to have rediscovered me, acquaintance of her childhood. In easy comfort we fell together. Maria (for that was her name) would not fall asleep that night and told me she was very happy. I must say that I felt the beginnings of happiness myself. In the morning we went out for breakfast.

Thus the arrangement continued for some time; I would go to her (spacious) apartment after work and we would eat dinner and dredge up memories of our childhood. "Remember the train station?" she would ask me. "Yes," I would respond. There were always magazines and paperbacks left in the waiting room by some citizens of the suburb; there was a sign there saying 'Take a book, leave a book.' I would go there sometimes to read, in the waiting room. Commuters would get off the trains in the evening and their loved ones would be waiting for them.

Maria was kind to me. On my birthday she booked a cabin on a lake three hours out of the city, and she excelled herself in giving me pleasure that day. Every day I had been feeling slightly more happy. But on my birthday, she came out with her gift. It was a gold-plated shaving kit. I wept, because it had been a long time since anyone had given me a gift. Oh, there were my clients at the firm, of course, who sent me bottles of whiskey in appreciation of my services, but I had an inkling that this was different. I put the cold gold against my cheek. It felt nice. I apologised for being lachrymose, and held the hand of Maria. The next day I sent her a note by courier. She was not the One.

The third individual with whom I became intimate was my wife. Of her I do not care to speak; marriage is an offence against love.

The fourth was the woman who set off the concatenation of happenstance that has brought my life to its present pass. She was a lady of the evening or a woman of pleasure. I made her acquaintance on a business trip. She was sent up to my room as a goodwill gesture by the client I was servicing. She came into my hotel room and proceeded to dispose of her garments, repose on the bed, and regard me with a frank, inviting look. I sat opposite her and ascertained the purpose of her salacious display. Then I informed her, not without some heat, that I was not in need of her ministrations, that I should be taking the matter up in the morning with my client as well as with my superiors in the firm, that she was insulting the dignity of her sex by disporting herself thus.

At this the professional woman—Vicki—burst into tears.

She responded to my diatribe by saying, between sobs, that she didn't know why she did this, she had a child to support, it was hard for her to pretend to be sexually excited by businessmen in hotel rooms whom she otherwise would not give the time of day to. When she had finished weeping, she clasped my hand and earnestly pleaded with me not to inform my client, because she would then be rationalised from her agency and be deprived of her livelihood. The agency, she explained, would put the burden of blame onto her, assuming that she was insufficiently versed in the erotic arts. She requested that I permit her to spend the next fifty minutes in my room, since her driver cum minder was waiting for her in the lobby of the hotel and would report her to her agency if she left early. Saying all this, Vicki clutched my arm and beheld me with the face of one seeking urgent assistance.

I was swayed by the genuine alarm and apprehension in her voice. It would not discombobulate me to allow her to pass fifty minutes in my room, as long as she was decently clothed, so I offered her a fortified beverage from the refrigerator in the room, and sat at a discreet distance from her. Every man has some curiosity about the lifestyle of these women who have been peddling their trade since the dawn of time but who have always been the subject of reprobation from society. Although, from an accounting standpoint, she was providing a legitimate service to satisfy a basic need in exchange for a pre-set fee. Her services, because illegal, fell outside the scope of the taxation laws, and thus there was not much room for an accountant in her profession. I could not interrogate her on the structure of her income-tax returns. Hence, I proceeded to put to her questions about the process of her recruitment and training in her profession.

Sitting on the bed, Vicki informed me that she had a male companion, or boyfriend, to whom she was extraordinarily attached. She had met him in one of her educational institutions, and they had set up a conjugal household and produced the child out of wedlock. This boyfriend, unhinged by so much responsibility at a very early age, had fallen upon an undesirable set of acquaintances, who introduced him to powerful hallucinogens. Although Vicki herself abstained from these mind-altering substances, she had to furnish him with the finances to procure the expensive pharmaceuticals, for he threatened to part ways with her if she did not. In a left-wing tabloid, whose feminist articles in the front were subsidised by the pornographic advertisements in the back, she spotted a commercial notice offering high wages for women of exceptional beauty. This description correctly applied to her. When she went for her interview, she could discern at a glance that it was a house of ill fame. The madam of the establishment sent her on a variety of calls, to expensive hotels, to bachelor parties, and to business conferences. Vicki loathed her work, but she dreaded even more the thought of never seeing her boyfriend again. He was aware of the extreme distress she underwent to buy him his needs, and abused her roundly for her work while taking

her money without demur. The child watched these scenes from
the door of her room silently. It occurred to me that Vicki had built
up a dependency on her boyfriend just as surely as he had upon his
narcotics. This occurred to me, but I did not mention it at the time
to this young woman speaking to me from across the room in calm,
measured tones.

It was a tale that aroused distress and sympathy in me, and I
thought it genuine and not calculated. She had asked nothing of
me other than that she be allowed to spend fifty minutes in my
room. When that time was over, she got up to leave. I thanked her
and, shaking her hand, bid her farewell.

However, when I got back to my home and my wife, I could not
erase the memory of that encounter. As I went about my well-
defined tasks, I found some part of my mind dwelling on Vicki's
plight. I recalled that she put her hand to her mouth, quickly, for
just an instant, when she recounted some particularly distressing
detail in her sad saga, such as the time she came home and found
that her child, alone and unsupervised, had bled from a cut and
had constructed a makeshift bandage fashioned from her Snoopy
blanket. Her child, Vicki recalled, with that quick movement of
the hand, had met her with the large blanket trailing from her
arm. It was perhaps the first time in my life that I had had such
direct experience of immense human suffering, and it would not
be too much to say that if affected me deeply. I resolved to furnish
assistance to this woman.

Accordingly, I telephoned the client who had dispatched her to
me. If a voice over the telephone could be said to contain a knowing smirk, my client's voice had one. He inquired whether I had
had a "good time" during my visit to his town. Playing his game, I

responded that I had, in fact, had a "very good" time. Thereupon, this client commenced on a series of coarse remarks and double entendres, asking me if I had used the "double-entry" system; if my books were balanced now; how my bottom line was; if my technique had conformed to FASB standards, etc. He punctuated each witticism with a hearty guffaw. I waited for him to calm down. Then I asked of him the phone number of the agency where the woman might be procured again, declaring that that one night had taken me into new frontiers of the erotic, that I had felt moved and shaken and wished to repeat the experience. Pleased that I had been pleased, my client promptly gave me the number, which he seemed to have committed to memory.

Telephoning the agency, I requested them to deliver my favoured demimondaine, Vicki, to me in my city for an evening. I would, of course, pay for the transportation and fully recompense them for her time in transit. I might ask myself, said the accountant, why I did not simply ask the agency to give her ten thousand dollars on my behalf. Perhaps, he answered, I was afraid that the agency would appropriate the charitable contribution themselves. Or perhaps, he continued, I wanted to give her the money personally, gratify some ignoble urge in myself to see her face aglow with gratitude as I presented her with the wherewithal to make a fresh start in her star-crossed life.

In any case, on the following evening, I drove to the airport and picked up Vicki, taking her to the nearest respectable hostelry. Once in the room, I sat across the table from her and told her I had been struck by her predicament, and had carefully considered possible avenues of egress. It would have been simple for me, I informed her, to merely have turned over an appropriate sum of money to her, but there was always the possibility that she might just turn over the check to her boyfriend, out of a mistaken assumption that this might buy his love once and for all.

Vicki listened impassively.

Therefore, I continued, I had resolved to compensate her for not taking specific outcalls that the agency sent her on. I asked her how many calls she would go on in a typical week, and she guessed about twenty; therefore, I said, I would pay her for each client that she did not service. Anytime, I told her, the noisome reality of her chosen profession became too much for her, she was to keep records of the evening, and I would fully compensate her for her lost income. And what was she to do with that time? She should not tell her boyfriend about our little arrangement; she could spend her free time with her child, or reading an improving book, or going to the moving pictures, or whatever leisure activity she chose. This arrangement, I informed her, would continue till she had exhausted the provident fund of twenty thousand dollars.

Vicki seemed to be having some difficulty grasping the nature of my proposal. "And what d'you want me to do for you?" she asked.

"Keep detailed records," I answered.

I saw her back to the aerodrome that very evening, and thought no more about her for some time. Then, about a month later, she telephoned me. "I couldn't do it last night," she said, simply. She revealed to me that her procuress had inquired of her whether she would service a new client, a German man of affairs, who was possessed of a curious fetish. This personage, it seemed, wished to imbibe substantial quantities of beer and then micturate upon attractive women. He was prepared to pay generously for the privilege and Vicki needed the money; her child required medical attention for some infection. But she found the prospect of being drenched with the businessman's efflux unappealing, and hence inquired of me whether I would compensate her for not taking the call. I acceded with alacrity.

Thus began my education in the shadowed side of human sexuality. Every so often, Vicki would communicate with me by telephone or postal letter, recording the precise nature of the customer's request that she had declined or wished to refuse. There were the men who wished to inflict physical pain on her, with the aid of various implements or just with their bare hands. There were necrophiliacs, coprophiliacs, zoophiliacs, and sitophiliacs. Then there were those who wanted to arrange a copulatory session involving Vicki, themselves, and other interested parties such as their wives, best friends, business colleagues, manservants, and, in one case, a specially trained armadillo. Vicki's feeling was that two was a sufficient and necessary number in any amatory exercise. Concurring with her estimate, I duly compensated her for refusing.

At one point, Vicki's withdrawals from the fund demonstrated particularly strong activity. In the course of one bad week, she requested recompense for declining to service a Congressman who wished to use her body as a candelabra, decorating it with lit candles prior to entering it; a precious-metals trader desirous of a form of intercourse prohibited by all major world religions; and a surgeon who did not specify the services he required of her but caressed a set of steel surgical instruments meditatively as she undressed. These three payments depleted the fund by an appreciable percentage, and, as her accountant, I felt it my fiduciary responsibility to inform her that, should this sudden spurt in deviance not prove to be temporary, the money would run out in a matter of weeks. Switching roles and speaking as her benefactor, I inquired of her whether she had sought alternate employment, involving parts of her body other than the orificial. Perhaps I was a bit harsh, for I heard prolonged sounds of distress at the other end of the line. Feeling remorseful, I decided to fly to her town and provide her gustatory comfort by cooking for her my reputed asparagus and rabbit casserole. I had manufactured this savoury edible before for the Cuban woman, for Maria, and for my duly married wife when she had first granted me her final favour.

It was a matter of some surprise to myself that I found myself purchasing provenance in the anticipation of creating this same baked delight for Vicki; I realised that she had come to occupy some appreciable space in the circle of people I wished well. Having acquired the lapine raw material, I flew to Vicki's town and hired conveyance to her professional establishment.

I was shown into a tastefully appointed parlour by a woman whose garb and deportment betrayed no trace of the sweaty purpose of the enterprise that she fronted for; she could have been one of the administrative assistants at my own firm. Unlike the images out of old Westerns that come to mind when one imagines a house of ill-repute, there were no amply fleshed ladies lounging around the player piano in a state of dishabille, no raucous madam urging the clientele on to drink and debauchery. No, I was intrigued to observe, this was run as a staid, even august, business operation; they could have been offering for sale real estate, magazines, soft drinks or computer software—but of course, what was on the block was Woman. The office looked, in fact, exactly like a temporary employment agency. Can True Love flourish here? I mused. Is this where bridges are crossed, between myself and the Other?

While waiting for my chosen hoyden, I engaged the secretary in conversation. In all innocence, she made certain revelations, divulged particular confidences.

Presently Vicki emerged, clothed in a dress whose progress upward toward her neck and downward toward her knee had been interrupted well short of those goals. I could not tell if she was pleased or flustered to behold me. The efficient manageress at the reception desk established a temporary lien on my credit card, and Vicki led me into a bedroom, or chamber of sexual union, that looked exactly like an upscale motel room. It was furnished in subdued pastels and hanging over the bed was an amorphous painting of what was either clouds, misted-over mountain tops, or amoebae magnified under a microscope. Nothing about the room gave one the impression that bodily secretions would soon stain the sheets, and the walls would echo with guttural cries of inchoate passion. As in our previous encounter, I took a chair by the window, and Vicki reposed on the vast bed.

I pulled out from my briefcase the now unfrozen rabbit meat and offered it to her in the manner of a gift. The woman blanched. "We're gonna eat Bugs Bunny!" I sallied jocularly. Vicki crawled backwards from the bed, away from me, on all fours. "You've been lying to me!" I set the rabbit meat in flight at her. The package missed her and bounced off the wall. I was standing up by now. My clothes were coming off. "I wanna get my money's worth. Twenty thousand dollars worth."

It was a day of prolonged sexual conjunction; it would not be too much to say that we rutted. I was seized, as never before, by sexual desire. Was it vengeance I was seeking as our bodies joined at midpoint? I wanted to enact in real life all her imagined perversities, which she had so dramatically and starkly described for my benefit in the past few months. I wanted to beat her with a rubber hose, I wanted to invite my mother in for the ceremonies, I wanted to push small furry animals into her orifices. As I thrust into her, I found myself arriving at the conjunction of lust, pain, and money. This person writhing beneath me was no human; she was a purchase, duly paid for, and if I could fudge it on my expense reports, tax-deductible.

In the end, Cupid's arrow lost its ardour, and I withdrew, curled into a foetal position, and sucked my thumb. I felt Vicki's lips just below my eyelids, kissing the water away as she caressed my hair. It was almost sisterly. Through the pressure of her cheek on mine I discovered that hers, too, was bedewed.

"Where is True Love?" I asked.

"Anywhere but here," she answered.

Since that stressful encounter, a mutually non-obligatory friendship developed between me and Vicki. We call each other every few weeks, and she is my advisor in my pursuit of True Love, teaching me to look for the salient features that distinguish the veritable from the mendacious. I send her no money; I am no longer her patron, and she does not have to concoct saturnalia for my delectation. In fact, both of us pointedly circumlocute the subject of her work. I have no doubt that she is still engaged as a harlot, that she provides sustenance for herself and her progeny through morally reprehensible means, but that is none of my concern. On Bell's invention, we converse on other matters, such as the progress of her child, the proper way to baste a guinea hen, and, of course, my continuing, episodic search for True Love. For my encounter with Vicki had made me realise that there was a lacuna in my marriage. It is correct to say that I was 50% partner in an enterprise of wedlock with my spouse. But that arrangement had not, regrettably, satiated my thirst for True Love, and thus I looked outside the domiciliary purview, late one night in the apartment of a woman named Jenny.

Jenny had put some kind of music on, some woeful ballad, for me to be aroused by while she bedecked herself with birth control. Coming to the boudoir, Jenny sat at the edge of the bed tentatively. Being as she was an acquaintance of my wife as well as of myself, she had become thoughtful in the bathroom, as women are wont to, about what might ensue. I advanced upon her to quell doubt. Nuzzling her ears, probing her mouth, I demonstrated urgent need for congress. She began reciting a list of reasons for us to desist, and I interrupted her, informing her that I was well aware already of all of them. Then I spoke to her of the joy of flesh meeting flesh, of my established expertise in conjugal connection, of the neurologically stimulating experience I was confident of providing her with. Jenny remained unmoved. She stated that she wished to desist from the physical expression of love with anyone for a while, having but recently recovered from a turbulent liaison with a faithless partner. Not being one to thrust my affections unwanted upon anyone, I complied. For a while we clung together in a demonstration of friendship, periodically interrupted by my renewed kisses, but every time my fingers would steal to her forbidden parts, her hand would grip mine. It was evident that the woman desired slumber rather than union. Finally, I removed myself to another mattress in the same chamber, and lay supine upon it. Neither of us enjoyed restful repose that night. Ere dawn, I rose, performed minimal ablutions, and stole away from Jenny's apartment. I enjoy her acquaintance to this day, but the boundaries were set during that encounter. We could know each other, but not as partners in that act whose original purpose, long since lost in our fallen world, was procreation.

It was this selfsame Vicki who put me on guard against my marital partner. My wife had been going on ever-extending business trips, returning to our abode of primary residence long after middle-class people retire for the evening. I suspected nothing. But, on our telephonic exchanges, Vicki would enquire, "It's ten o'clock. Do you know where your wife is, you sap?" I told her I assumed she was detained by some errand of moment. But then, guided by the wise courtesan, I started looking for signs of adulterous liaisons. I noticed that all the volumes of poetry had been removed from the top shelf of the bookcase. And, what, pray tell, was that mysterious smile that kept playing about the corner of her mouth? After she would come back and fall into the arms of Morpheus, I would creep into the bathroom, open the laundry basket, and check her unmentionables for traces of human seed. Twice I found yellowing stains, but the origin of the emissions, whether excretory or replicatory, I could not ascertain. What was I doing there, I asked myself, standing at three o'clock in the morning secreted in a bathroom, holding a woman's used underwear, looking for the space between the word and the act? O what, the accountant asked himself, sinking to the tiles still holding the lace cloth, has become of True Love and what has become of my fair bride and what will become of me?

I became distracted by phantoms; while at the office poring over my commodious ledgers, I saw the tortured bodies of my wife and a host of virile amourants coiling and uncoiling across the blank pages. Then it happened: I made an error. A client in the Southwest who needed to depreciate the value of an oil well found to his discomfiture that I had actually appreciated it. In the salty language favoured by those of his province when in dudgeon, the client brought this lapse to my attention. It was the first time in all my years at the firm that I had slipped, and I felt bludgeoned. Going home, I faced the perfidious wench, arms akimbo. "Confess!" I screamed.

I shall not go into the soiled details of the incident that ensued; the records are available in the police station for anyone desirous of perusing them. Suffice it to say that I found myself on the telephone later that evening, in an excess of lament, revealing all, withholding nothing, to Vicki. Wasn't what I entertained for my spousal partner True Love? The constabulary at the scene would, if their views were solicited, assuredly beg to differ. Or perhaps they wouldn't. For what we did to each other, the officers of the law must know, vast as their knowledge of the shadows between one human being and the other is, indicates not the absence of True Love but its raging presence, its grotesque and feral torrent.

It is now the sunrise of the morning after and I have my head and my life in my hands. There is this elation that fills my being, this apprehension and this exhilarated sadness—the light comes in through the six small windows of this room and converges in the centre. The walls and floors of the bedroom, in which I sit, are festooned with the traces of the objects that we employed as missiles last night. I feel like dancing; yes here I am going, you can see me, going over to the stereo to put on this urgently libidinal music; here, I am dancing. I watch myself in the mirror. I say my name. I say it as each of my women, at climax, called out to me, each in a different way, with different accents, each stressing a different part of it—I say all of my names, one by one, over and over.

AMITAVA KUMAR

Indian Restaurant

SHASTRIJI was my neighbour. His apartment was on Westcott. I live on Forster Avenue, and Westcott is the next street on the way to the university. I think Shastriji came here in '84, but I cannot be sure. When I met Shastriji six months ago, I liked going to his apartment. It was like visiting a friend's house in Bihar. He always asked me if I'd like to have tea, but I never came away without eating dinner.

Our first meeting was in the library. I was sitting in the periodicals section. I had seen him looking at me. He was a middle-aged man, slightly heavy, wearing a blue denim shirt tucked into his khaki pants. With his good clothes and small paunch, he looked respectable. I had never seen him before. When I saw him walking towards me, I knew he wanted the *Outlook* I was reading. He came and stood near me.

When I looked up, he smiled sheepishly. He didn't ask me to give him the magazine. He only said: "Excuse me, is it the latest one?"

I didn't know if it was or not. I showed him the cover with Sonia Gandhi on it. She was wearing a nice sari, but it seemed she had grown older in just two years.

Shastriji said: "I have already read that. They still haven't got the new one."

I said, "Maybe there is a postal strike in India."

He grinned, showing his teeth. "These days all the magazines are sent by computer. And then printed in New Jersey or Chicago. So, that wouldn't affect it." I didn't know this. He extended his hand and introduced himself. I did the same. He heard my name and asked, "You are from U.P.?"

"No, Bihar."

This time he grinned more broadly. His gums were dark, like his skin. This darkness made his eyes and teeth more striking.

Shastriji said, "I am too."

He asked, "From Patna?"

I nodded.

"Let's go have tea," he said.

In the university cafetaria, there were five types of coffee, and only one kind of tea. The girl behind the counter had her right eyebrow pierced with a ring. When she gave us the tea, she put the tea-bag in hot-water, dumped some sugar, and then poured the milk immediately over it. As a result, the tea remained very light and watery. Shastriji grinned again. He did not seem at all self-conscious about his dark gums and the peeling skin on his fingers. I liked him.

After Shastriji said a few things about Patna, I guessed he was about ten years older than me, somewhere around forty. He lived with his wife and two children, a son and a daughter. He was about to complete his M.A. in South Asian Studies. He had earlier taught for a short period in Allahabad after getting an M.A. in English. I asked him if his wife worked. He said, "Arre, ladies...." And he looked at me, as if I understood everything. Although I didn't, I wanted to, and I said "Yes ... yes."

Shastriji did not look worried when I told him I had managed to come on an exchange-student visa arranged for me by the secretary of the Education Department and of course I was interested in seeing if there was any scope of staying longer. He kept nodding his head vigorously while I talked, even though his eyes wandered away sometimes.

When women passed our table, he would suddenly jerk his head up and look at them straight in the eye. A couple of times, the women would slow down thinking he knew them or was going to say something. I found this intriguing rather than irritating.

We got up after having finished our tea. He took my phone number and then he said he would call me. I could drink real tea in his home, he said. I shook hands with him.

"What is your father's name?" Shastriji asked me before letting go of my hand. I answered him.

Then, he said, "And your mother's family is from Patna too? What is your mother's title?"

In America, they always say "last name." When I heard Shastriji use the word "title" it took me back home. Later on, however, I got the feeling that he had wanted to find out about my caste, but I cannot be certain about this.

Shastriji's father had been the Post-Master in Patna. I must have heard his name when I lived at home. Every morning my father read out the names of all the officials in the news stories printed in the Patna edition of *Hindustan Times*.

"B.K. Singh has been tranferred again."

"K.N. Das has been moved back to Supply."

"Rameshwar babu is still holding on. Bahut stubborn aadmi hai."

The decision against *The Times of India* was taken in our household because the regional editor is a Bengali. The editor of *Hindustan Times* is from our own caste. It is true that we do not know him personally, but my uncle said the editor might even be related to us.

By the time two cups of tea had been drunk, and the whole newspaper read, my father was ready to proclaim: "It is useless to talk about this, this is only what can happen in Laloo's raj...." When I left India, Laloo Yadav was still the Chief Minister of Bihar. Now, it is his wife who is in that office; Laloo is in and out of prison these days.

I am sure I heard the name of Shastriji's father on some of those mornings. It used to annoy me to hear my father go on with his list, but it is now one of the things I miss about home.

I have been living in this country for the past two years. Everyone tells me that the first years are the ones during which you have to struggle the most. I think that is natural. I did not see a bright future for myself in Bihar. Some people said to me that I should go to Delhi. But everyone was leaving for Delhi. Even the servants wanted to go there. I heard our servant Mantu one day talking about Palika Bazaar.

So, I stayed behind. When the chance came to come to America, I took it. And I have been happy here. It is not very cold, except in winter. Three months after my arrival, I bought a coat for sixty five dollars and also boots and gloves. Cooking is a bit of a problem, but you can buy rice that is ready in a minute. It is called Minute-Rice. I think my English has improved. I'm less worried about money now.

I had come home that evening and was cutting cauliflower for my dinner when the phone rang. My room-mate was Esra, an African man. I let him pick up the phone because he got most of the calls but he said it was for me.

It was Shastriji. He said, "Were you cooking?"

"No, no, I was just washing my face," I said. I might have lied because I thought I would not be invited to his apartment if I said I was cooking.

Shastriji said, "Why don't you come over for tea?"

"Right now?" I said.

He said, "Yes, yes. It is only two minutes away. The kettle is already on the stove."

I had hoped the invitation would be for dinner. It was already seven in the evening. "Okay," I said.

"Theek hai," he said. And added, "No formality."

Shastriji's wife and children were waiting behind the door. I was introduced to them.

Shastriji's wife was perhaps my age. She was tall and a little thin. Her face was pretty. She was dressed in a simple cotton sari but she had put on lipstick to look more presentable. Her name was Madhu. She folded her hands in greeting and said, "I have seen you walking to the university several times." From the way she spoke, it was clear that she was also from Bihar.

I learned the names of the children, Manav and Chitra. Chitra had pink butterflies clipped to her hair and she clung to her mother's sari. The boy said, "Uncle, do you want to see my website?" Shastriji laughed and shooed him off. I kept standing. Madhu went to get the tea. The kitchen was on the other end of the room. This was a graduate student apartment owned by the university. A large dining table took much of the space.

Shastriji gestured toward the small sofa nearby. "Sit down," he said. He himself sat on the carpet, his legs folded under him. There was a pile of newspapers behind him. I was impressed that he bought papers here. *The New York Times* cost a whole dollar and I only picked it up in the university cafetaria when people left it on the table.

I said, "The newspapers in America are thicker than the Patna phone directory."

Shastriji laughed. He said, "People don't talk to each other here. That is why they need such thick papers."

When Madhu brought the tea, Shastriji said, "Your bhabhi wanted to meet you."

She smiled and said, "He did not even ask you whether you were married!"

I had been to three Indian homes since coming to America. At each place, I was asked this question in the first ten minutes; I was happy I had identified a national trait. I said, "My mother is worried that I will marry a white girl here."

Madhu said, "Do you know Atul?" I did not know who she was talking about. Shastriji said, "He's from Banaras. Nice boy. Statistics."

Madhu said, "He has got a black girlfriend. Cynthia. Baap re baap, think of what his mother will say." I had seen an Indian with a black woman on campus; last year, they had also come together for the Diwali festival on the College Greens. Now I knew who they were.

Later, when Shastriji and I were talking, Madhu came and asked me, "Do you like vegetarian or non-vegetarian?" I turned to Shastriji. I said, "I was just about to start cooking when you called."

"No, no. You eat here," he said.

"I had taken the chicken out from the fridge," I lied again. "I should go. Some other time."

They were both persistent in a nice way and I stayed back for dinner. Madhu went to the far end, where the stoves were, and began cooking.

Shastriji lit a cigarette and said, "Do you take anything alcoholic?"

He sounded a bit uncomfortable asking the question. So, I said, "Sometimes."

He got up and said without any fuss, "Let's have some whiskey." I kept sitting while Shastriji padded across, barefoot, to his fridge. In front of me was a framed poster of a Festival of India exhibition in Chicago. Madhu was frying onions. She had placed a pressure cooker on the second stove.

When Shastriji brought a bottle of Johnny Walker and two glasses with ice, I said, "I haven't had a chance to go to many bars yet."

"No need to," he said. While he unscrewed the bottle, the cigarette was clutched between his lips. The smoke made him screw-up his eyes. Madhu came into the part of the room where we were sitting, picked up a pair of shoes from the floor, and then climbed the stairs without saying anything to us.

"Why should we go to bars?" Shastriji asked. But, he didn't answer the question. I stayed silent.

I took my glass and said "Cheers."

He said, "To Bihar." And laughed.

I was hungry and the first sip of the whiskey cut into my stomach like sharp glass. But, it felt good. I began feeling light-headed. There was music playing on the stereo in the corner and Shastriji hit the repeat button when the Mastt-Mastt song from *Mohra* had reached its end.

Shastriji said, "Do you go to coffee houses? There's a great culture here of coffee houses... But I don't like bars. I like drinking at home."

"Yes," I said.

A little later we had dinner. There was chhola and mutton, with raita on the side. Madhu also made puris. I had not eaten a puri for at least a year. I ate the food greedily, but so did Shastriji. I did not feel very bad about my gluttony. Madhu joined us when we were finishing up. She asked me a few questions about my sisters. After dinner, Shastriji stretched his legs out on the carpet and lit another cigarette.

We decided to have another drink. The kids could be heard in the room upstairs. I heard Madhu's voice talking to them. What would I call her? Madhu or Bhabhi? She was attractive but a little withdrawn. I think she was lonely.

"Why would you want to go to bars?" Shastriji asked. The drink was making him repeat himself, but I didn't mind.

"For the experience," I said.

Some time passed. Then, as if I still needed to explain something, I added, "I would like to have a drink in a proper bar. To be served cocktails."

Shastriji nodded and then I became conscious that the music had stopped a while ago.

"When I was in Patna," Shastriji spoke in the silence, raising his right arm above him, "when the barber came...after shaving me, he would take his razor and shave my armpits."

He said, "You can't get that kind of service here. So, why go to bars? Eat well and drink well at home, and be happy."

We had Halloween in November. I dressed up as Dracula for Manav and Chitra. They liked it when I laughed loudly and showed my fangs. Both of the kids wore small plastic masks. I noticed that even when children are wearing Halloween masks, you can so easily read the fear in their eyes and shapeless mouths.

I took Manav and Chitra trick-or-treating to every door in our neighbourhood. Madhu had dressed Chitra in a pink lehenga with gold embroidery; she thought an Indian dress worked fine as a Halloween costume. When people gave candy to Chitra, they said things like, "Oh, look! An Indian princess."

Two days after Halloween, I got a call at home from Shastriji. Madhu's father had died. She had got the news that morning from India. "Massive heart-attack," Shastriji said on the phone. Madhu's father had been a well-to-do farmer in Purnea and ran a small publishing business. I went over to Westcott at once. Madhu had wiped all the make-up from her face and was wearing her long black hair loose. Her eyes looked unnaturally large. She had been crying.

I did not know what to say when I was in front of her. Shastriji smoked cigarettes and lowered his voice whenever Madhu came downstairs.

He told me that the Indian Students Association was going to invite Naseeruddin Shah to visit our campus. The actor was on a tour of the U.S. This was exciting news. Shastriji was not very optimistic. He thought that the Indians who held office in the Association were stupid and elitist.

He said, "English-speaking Doon School types. Rambo ke aulaad hain. They wouldn't know Naseeruddin Shah even if he was their father."

Madhu came down once again. She looked at me and asked me if I was very busy. I said no. She said, "Can you get some of your friends to come for dinner next Saturday? It will be for babuji, for the peace of his soul. I should feed six of you."

I said, "Sure."

Shastriji and Madhu were Brahmins. I was not. In their family in Patna, I am certain that it was unmarried Brahmin youth who would have been fed after a ceremony. But, how were they going to get so many Brahmins here? Both of them had clearly discussed this already and it was okay with them. I didn't mind. I got five others—only two of them Indian—to come with me for dinner. Half of them were American students from my own Sociology department, eager to eat Indian food; the others were desi students I had met during the Orientation Week at International House.

We gathered in front of Willard Building and then walked to Shastriji's place. The apartment always smelled of food, but today the smell was especially welcoming. On the stereo, Bhimsen Joshi was singing bhajans. Shastriji wore a white kurta over his jeans. He looked freshly bathed.

Madhu had made fish because her father liked it. There was

basmati rice and potato cutlets. Madhu said she looked for curd but the yogurt they sold here was nothing like the curds that her father loved. So, she was giving us spoonfuls of sour cream from its plastic container. It was very rich and went well with the food. She served us gulab jamuns at the end.

Shastriji didn't join us for dinner. While the guests were having their gulab jamuns, he sat down on the table with a heaped plate of food. I went and sat next to him. He asked me, "Mazaa aaya?"

I nodded. Sometimes, at Shastriji's house, I surprised myself by my appetite. I now wanted some whiskey, but I did not know whether it would be appropriate. Did Madhu's father like whiskey? Shastriji said he had to take a driving test the next day. While chewing on the food, he asked me if I could come with him.

At the driving licence office, they wanted Shastriji to take a written test first. We needed to consult a manual for that purpose. I didn't have a licence, although I used to have one in India. Shastriji had never driven before. I decided to take the test with him.

Both of us stood in front of computer terminals and touched the screen to answer yes or no to questions. The questions were from the manual. "If there are two yellow lines in the middle of the street, is it permitted to cross the line?" Shastriji bit his lip and often refused to make up his mind about the right response. Now and again, he would ask me for the answer in Hindi. I helped him. He did not know what "double parking" meant. This required a more detailed explanation. I looked around and began answering, but stopped when I saw a blonde who was wearing thick glasses looking at us.

I passed; Shastriji failed. He tried again the following week and did well. We had to return for the driving test. This test was more difficult. Shastriji had only driven around in a parking lot with his Chilean friend, Ricardo. The examiner was a tall, black man wearing dark glasses. He was very dignified and didn't waste any words. In his right hand, he carried a clipboard. Shastriji became nervous and started speaking to him in Hindi. The examiner turned to look at me but didn't say a word.

It was impossible to know what he was thinking. I looked at Shastriji and spoke to him in Hindi. I asked him, "Shall we let it be today?"

Shastriji quickly said, "Yes, let's go."

He looked back at the examiner and said to him in English, "Thank you." Neither of us got the licence. Shastriji came out of the building and lit his cigarette. He laughed loudly. He said, "Saala, America mein bahut tamaasha hai."

I returned by myself for the test later, after two or three weeks had passed. I got the licence in the mail a week before Christmas. Madhu said that when they had found a good second-hand car, I was to take her to the Mall for holiday shopping. I said yes. We had just finished eating in Shastriji's home.

Madhu laughed when I told her about Shastriji asking me questions in Hindi during the written test. Shastriji didn't seem to mind my revealing all this. He chuckled quietly from time to time as he listened to me telling Madhu our story. I didn't tell Madhu the part about his becoming nervous and beginning to speak to the examiner in Hindi.

Shastriji got up and went to the kitchen sink. Madhu said to him that he wasn't to wash any dishes. "There'll be no one worse than me if you do that," she said to him in Hindi. It was clear to me that she loved him very much.

Shastriji filled a glass with water. Then, he looked at me and said, "You should get married. You will not even have the freedom to drink water then." Madhu kept smiling. I remember thinking then that it was not only her love—she was also more patient with him than others were.

A few days later, I passed the Insomnia Coffee House and saw Shastriji inside sitting with an elderly man. The man had grey curling hair on the sides of his head. He gave me a limp hand when I was introduced to him. I noticed that Shastriji was not at ease, and kept speaking to me in English. I left a few minutes later.

Shastriji called me on the phone that night. That man was his Department Head. Shastriji was having some problems with his thesis supervisor. I asked him what the problem was and he replied vaguely, "Arre, politics." I began to hear from one or two desis that Shastriji did not do much writing. His teaching evaluations were also low. His situation in the university was turning precarious. The most effort Shastriji made toward getting a degree was to invite a faculty member for dinner at his house. A German graduate student in my department who was older than me twisted his mouth and said, "Your friend Shastri is going to have problems with any supervisor who doesn't like Indian food."

A month later when the accident took place, I think it gave Shastriji an excuse to go back to India. I have not heard from him since he left; my father wrote in a letter that he had run into Shastriji at a wedding and that he looked well. I often wonder about Shastriji and ask myself if he had really failed in America. Wasn't there a part of him that could only be happy back in India, in Bihar? He had gone back home.

All the others who succeeded in this country did so only by changing. They became someone else. Shastriji, for good or bad, never did. I don't know why he hasn't written to me. Perhaps that too is a sign of his not having changed. But, sometimes, I wonder whether Madhu blames me for the accident. I want her to write to me someday.

Shastriji had bought the old Volvo from someone in his department four days after New Year's day. It was after he had already bought his car that he succeeded in getting his licence. It was freezing cold during those days. The first day we only talked on the phone. On the second day, however, Shastriji called again. He had a plan. The university hadn't reopened, so I too had nothing to do. I walked over to his house. He said, "Let's take a drive in the parking lot."

We stood on the road with our hands in our pocket and inspected the car. It was old but looked okay. The blue of the paint had faded and some parts of the car looked rusty. The tyres would need to be changed. Then, we got in. Shastriji said that the steering wheel was a little slow. But, the heater worked and it was comfortable in the car. We took it around the neighbourhood and then the parking lot where during the academic season all the buses idled.

On the way back, Shastriji double-parked in front of the corner grocery store run by a Lebanese man, Joe. Leaving me in the car, Shastriji hurried in to get his packet of Marlboros. When he came back, he said, "Achha, if you leave your emergency lights on when you double park, will the police still give you a ticket?"

I said I didn't know and I took a cigarette from Shastriji. It felt good to smoke in that cold. Shastriji said, "There is only one advantage to driving: we won't need to walk in the cold to the grocery store anymore." I looked at the peeling skin around his fingers as he clutched the steering wheel.

The car wasn't used much. Shastriji drove it to the grocery store with Madhu and once, when I was there, to the Mall to buy two sweaters and a new blender. Shastriji drove rather slowly, and people, as they sped by, sometimes looked back at us.

Shastriji did not care. While driving, he kept looking at me in the rear-view mirror as he spoke. Our talking made Madhu uncomfortable. As a rule, she sat next to Shastriji in the front. She kept saying, "Keep your eyes on the road."

But, Shastriji was not one for listening to such advice. I was only rarely bothered by this; being with Shastriji meant not giving the rest of the world much heed. It was as if we were back in Bihar. In the car that day, Shastriji was telling me about a man in his department who had gone to India as a hippie.

His name was Larry Drieker. Shastriji spelled his name out for me, the ringed index finger of his right hand rising above the steering wheel. He said, "Wherever Larry Drieker went in India, he found out that Indians everywhere called him Lorry Driver. Kashmir se Kanya Kumari tak...." Shastriji and I laughed.

I had noticed that I laughed a lot at Shastriji's stories, even when they were not very funny. When I spent time at their apartment, I would try to be spirited and full of stories. Madhu loved my tales, particularly when they involved details about how young American women behaved. I think, somewhere in my heart, I felt I needed to earn the food I ate so greedily at their table.

In February, Shastriji wanted to travel to Chicago. His passport was to be renewed at the Indian consulate. Perhaps he had already decided that they were going back to India. When they mentioned the trip to Chicago, they talked of going to India only for a visit. Madhu was excited. It seemed to me that a visit would erase the ache she had felt when she couldn't go home after her father's sudden death.

Madhu said, "You have not seen Chicago. Come with us." I said yes readily.

Shastriji said, "Chalo, chalo. We will eat good Indian food on Devon Street."

In spite of the cold, we went to the shores of Lake Michigan after our visit to the Indian consulate. The water was a freezing expanse of blue and white. After a minute, we ducked back in the Volvo. An Indian taxi-driver, with paan in his mouth, gave us directions to Devon Street. He called it Diwan Street.

It was two o'clock when we sat down for lunch. We ate hurriedly and we ate too much. Shastriji said, "Let's drink some beer for proper digestion." Madhu shook her head, but I was ready.

While we were drinking, Shastri asked Madhu to go the Gujarati store across the street and buy paan. When she was gone, he called the waiter. He said, "Please pack ten naans and two tandoori chicken. Please pack it quickly." On the way back, the car smelled of onion and the chicken. Madhu complained about the smell. Shastriji said, "At dinner-time tonight, you will be thanking me." Shastriji and I were sitting in the front; I was driving. When I looked at him, Shastriji laughed. The paan had turned his teeth red and they glistened under his dark gums.

We were still an hour away from home when a light freezing rain began to fall. The sun hadn't gone down and the light lit up

the valley to our left. The children were getting drowsy and irrita-
ble at the back. Madhu said to them, "Look." She was pointing at a
rainbow. It arched over the valley. A few cars passed with their
lights on, spraying our windscreen with water. Shastriji began
telling me about his old grandmother in Bhagalpur.

I cannot now remember what he was saying. All I remember is
his starting to talk about his grandmother standing on the roof of
her house and a rainbow above the Ganga. In the rain, the car
skidded first into the lane on the left. I must have braked very hard
when the car went out of control because under me I suddenly felt
the car spin around with a shriek. I thought we were going to hit
the rails in the middle of the highway.

Instead, in that long moment of spinning and shrieking, the car
seemed to float on water. I heard Madhu's voice behind me but I
don't know what she was saying. Then a pick-up van hit us smack
on the side and came to a stop. The car spun on impact and, for a
split second, it must have appeared as if we had parked next to the
van. Within that second, however, the truck which had been following the pick-up van had hit us from behind.

This time the car sped towards the rails on the right side. Glass
rained on me. For some absurd reason, I thought of the glass getting into the packets of tandoori chicken at the back. When we had
stopped, I tried feebly to open the car-door. I said, "Shastriji." I
heard nothing from my side. The children were screaming, it
seemed, in my ear. That noise mixed with the loud sound coming
from inside me. I was having trouble breathing. Not much time
had passed but it seemed that it was already evening.

And then, out of nowhere, I saw in front of me the face of my
elder sister in Patna. There were tears falling from her eyes. I

stayed with that face till I thought I heard the wailing sounds of the sirens which meant that the police, or perhaps the ambulance, had arrived.

When I saw them again, Shastriji was in the hospital. Madhu was in shock. Shastriji had to remain under close watch for four days because the cut on his head had worried doctors. Madhu and the children had small bruises and cuts. I had broken a rib where my chest had hit the steering wheel. The car would not be driven again.

Madhu's brother-in-law, Rakesh, a software engineer and industrialist in Delhi, happened to be in London for a fortnight. He came over to the U.S. for a weekend visit when he heard the news. Rakesh was a quiet man who spoke very elegant Hindi. One night we were together at the hospital and he took me to a Chinese restaurant for dinner; he sipped his beer methodically and spoke in English about the benefits of liberalization. He said things like, "If things keep going this way, in ten years there is no saying where India will be. India, not China, will be the sleeping giant that has at long last woken up."

Before Rakesh left, we had brought Shastriji home from the hospital.

A couple of nights later, I was sitting with Shastriji watching the late-night news on the TV. Shastriji turned to me and said that he was thinking of quitting smoking. I thought that this was a great idea. When Madhu came down after putting the children to sleep, I said to her, "Boss is thinking of quitting smoking."

Madhu came near us and said to me, "You should go home." I thought she was worried that I was overstraining myself; I said I was alright but would leave soon. She said, "No, I meant India." I became quiet, and nodded. I was surprised by her abruptness. Then, she said, "We should too." I didn't ask her why. I thought back to the time when her father had died. I remembered that Shastriji and I had talked about Naseeruddin Shah. Naseeruddin had fallen sick in Boston and was unable to come to our campus. At least Naseeruddin was now back in India.

I said, "Rakesh has the kind of money that makes living in America look like a stupid idea."

Madhu kept that calm expression of hers and said, "Money is never the reason why anyone says they are happy."

I could see that Madhu had changed. I remembered the evening I had taken her in their car to the Mall for what Madhu had called "holiday shopping." She must have picked up the phrase from the ads on radio or television. After we had finished buying the things she needed, Madhu asked me in Hindi, "Will you eat something?" I suddenly liked the idea of going to a restaurant alone with her. I said, "You eat, I'll have a beer."

There was a T.G.I. Friday inside the Mall. We went in and ordered some nachos with cheese. The beer was cheap. I was telling Madhu stories about being at a graduate student party one weekend. A woman named Eloise asked me to dance with her. I liked Eloise. I thought she was pretty. But, she also made me nervous. I didn't know how to dance. Awkwardly, I shuffled my feet and swayed my upper body to the music, as Eloise made encouraging noises. Madhu said, "What happened after that?" I shrugged. Nothing had happened but I wanted to tease Madhu with the thought that something might have transpired that evening between Eloise and me. I wanted her to think I was someone that women liked. She smiled. Madhu's smile always reached her eyes. I felt this was the best part about talking to her.

We went on talking and I ordered another beer. Then, the snow started to fall. The sight made us happy: it was as if we were back in India and the rain had begun to fall at the end of summer. I said this to Madhu and she began to talk of the rain in Purnea, how she would turn up her face to the clouds and feel the raindrops on her skin. I wanted to talk to Madhu about her childhood, but it was beginning to get late. In another half an hour it would be dark, and driving would be difficult.

When we stepped out of the Mall into the open, the sight of all the snow made me suddenly feel cold. And, impulsively, I drew closer to Madhu and she surprised me by taking my arm. The first thing I thought was that I hadn't ever touched her. And then I thought that we must appear to others right now as lovers. It might have been the beer I had drunk but I remember feeling very content with the pressure of Madhu's body at my side, her black hair so close to my mouth. Half an hour later, we were home with Shastriji and the children.

That evening seemed very distant now. Madhu was talking of going home and her voice betrayed an edge that I did not understand. I also began hearing from other people that Shastriji was going back to India. And then, Shastriji began to interrupt our own conversations to ask me whether I was coming back to Patna with them. He would say, "I will have a badminton court made in my garden. There we can play even in the winters."

I didn't find out whether Shastriji ever received his degree. There was no reason for me to ask him directly. It would have been rude. I heard Madhu saying to her Malaysian neighbour, "I am very happy that I came to this country. I am very happy that I am going back."

I decided I would ask Madhu more about this. But, as the day of their departure neared, there were more and more chores to do. I did everything I could to help them, buying boxes from U-Haul with my own money, and using them to pack all the children's toys and books in them. One night, Shastriji was playing a tape of S.D. Burman's music. I began talking about the actress Nutan, and how my mother used to like her. The film *Bandini* had been released when my mother was a young bride. She was alone in the village with her in-laws, and would sing the songs she had heard on the radio. When I said this, Madhu began to sob. Shastriji suddenly became serious. His face wore a pained expression. He did not even look at me. I could not even ask Madhu what was wrong. Our conversation had touched on some hurt or regret, and Shastriji seemed to be aware of it. All at once, I too wanted to go back home to Patna.

I often return to that moment when I remember them. It seems I have remained stuck there, while they have gone on to some place that I now know nothing about. I am still at the university. Next year, I will probably apply for admission to a doctoral program in Chicago. Only five weeks have passed since Shastriji left. Maybe Madhu will write me a letter. It is entirely possible Shastriji has mentioned this to Madhu a couple of times already. I can see him saying to her while drinking tea, "This is not nice. We should write him a letter. Why don't you write him a letter...?"

I was thinking of Shastriji when I was at Xanadu Cafe today. One afternoon, soon after Shastriji had bought the car, we were both sitting there. He was smoking and nodding his head the way he used to do while listening to me. He looked at the people walking in and out. It was so cold outside that the glass walls of the cafe had misted over. It seemed to me that with every word I spoke my breath froze on the glass.

Shastriji interrupted me and said, "Let's go to Shalimar. We'll digest some samosas. Mazaa aayega." Shastriji often said "digest" instead of "eating" and made the whole act appear very slow and leisurely.

I followed him out. As soon as I had stepped out, I regretted it. The cold instantly entered my bones. Shastriji was unfazed. Unlike me, he never wore gloves. He lit a cigarette. I said, "Why are we doing this for a wretched samosa?"

He said, "Jab tak rahega samosa mein aloo, Tab tak rahega Bihar mein Laloo."

The restaurant was a good ten minutes away. At last, we got there. The owner was a Pakistani, Javed. He welcomed us with a smile. He took Shastriji's hand in both his hands. When we sat down, Shastriji laughed and repeated, "Jab tak rahega samosa mein aloo, Tab tak rahega Bihar mein Laloo."

While we were waiting, Atul and his black girlfriend whose name I didn't remember walked in. Shastriji looked up and saw them. He grinned his black-gummed grin and waved them over to us.

Atul said, "Hello." I was introduced to him. He shook my hand.

Shastriji said, "Hello Cynthia, long time no see." She smiled and leaning forward kissed him on the right cheek. I was introduced to Cynthia. She said, "Very nice to meet you."

I was meeting Cynthia for the first time. She was beautiful and even her voice was a part of her allure. Cynthia spoke to Shastriji,

"So, how come you are here?"

Shastriji chuckled. When he laughed in an embarrassed way, his laugh struggled in his paunch. His laughter was a delaying tactic. Soon, he had an answer. He said, "We are celebrating the end of a politician called Laloo Yadav."

Cynthia looked puzzled. She glanced at Atul. Shastriji proceeded to explain the slogan he had been reciting: as long as there would be aloo or potato in the samosa, in Bihar we would have Laloo. He said, "But, in this restaurant, you get samosas with meat in it. So, we're celebrating Laloo's cultural demise."

Everyone smiled politely. We sipped our tea and waited for the samosas. When the food came, Shastriji continued in a philosophical vein. He stuffed his mouth with a samosa and said, "We have come to America and made something new. Look at you two, for example."

Atul and Cynthia smiled. Then, Cynthia turned her face to me. At this distance, you felt you could drown in her eyes. She said, "Are you from India? Or Pakistan?"

Before I could answer, Shastriji said, "What is the difference?"

Often, when I was in Shastriji's company, I was able to relax and just be myself. I think we both knew who we were when we were with each other. I didn't need to hide from him the fact that I didn't have an impressive record behind me or a future that was calling out to me; I was a youngish man from Bihar, single and somewhat aimless, stranded in this new land called America. Shastriji reminded me of my uncles. They put off things till tomorrow, and they knew that in some way tomorrow never comes. But, in front of strangers, Shastriji could affect a deep gravity. This was a part of his charm and it dawned on me later that this might have been the main reason why I spent so much time with him.

Shastriji had asked Cynthia that last question with a fine seri-ousness. He continued to smile faintly. Cynthia raised her lovely, plucked eyebrows. She said, "What is the difference? I don't know. You tell me."

Shastriji looked at her for a long moment and then, still smiling, began reciting the famous lines of Ali Sardar Jafri: "Tum aao gul-shan-e-Lahore se chaman bardosh, Hum aayen subh-e-Banaras ki roshnee le kar ..." He repeated the two lines because he could not recall what came next. Then, Shastriji mumbled a few words and said, "Aur iske baad yeh poochein ki kaun dushman hai?"

The words that Shastriji had remembered were delivered with a fine intensity. Cynthia had looked at Atul when Shastriji had mentioned Banaras. That was where Atul was from. She now asked Shastriji; "What does it mean?"

This was the woman who Shastriji as well as his wife were in some ways opposed to, and perhaps even looked down upon, because of the colour of her skin. But, I don't think Shastriji was the least conscious of his prejudice now. I cannot say whether it was a part of something new, or whether it was a return to an older, more dignified part of Shastriji's past. What I understood very clearly was that he had another sense of himself, and also of Cynthia, as he looked at her and smiled.

Shastriji nodded and took another drag from his cigarette. Then, once again affecting his noble charm, he translated Sardar Jafri's words for her in a very conversational way. He first looked at the restaurant-owner Javed in the corner and then pointed to Cynthia. He said: "You come to me laden with the flowers from the gardens of Lahore. I will come bearing the light of the morning of Banaras.... There is a line that I am forgetting.... After that, together we can ask, who is the enemy?"

There was a pause during which Shastriji drew on the cigarette. Cynthia was smiling. She waited a moment. Then, she said, "That's so beautiful."

AVTAR SINGH

Infected

'Infection' is just one of those words. Like its children, infected *and* infectious, *it doesn't have many friends. It grows up lonely, spends far too much time brooding, tries desperately and in the face of huge opposition to win others over to its peculiar purposes, and when it births itself on the outside world, accompanied by sores and fevers and other unpopular entities, carries with it the burden of malevolence and morbidity and contagion.*

Most people tend to avoid the infected. *Some people even avoid the word.*

You would think people are lonely enough these days, without worrying about catching it from someone else.

1.1

They talk on the phone a lot. Through the day, during the night. Sometimes through the night. She calls him when he's in the gym: he calls her back when he's finished. He speaks to her when she's at work. She seldom puts him on hold, though her job is an important one.

He is a filmmaker. A man with a little talent and a lot of ambition and very little hair left on his head. He is sensitive about this, and he works out a lot, she laughs to him sometimes in the middle of the night, because he is making up for his baldness. Though he doesn't think this is true, he laughs as well. Partly out of tiredness, partly to be polite, mostly because he doesn't want to hang up.

She is a consultant on management issues to large businesses. She has never run a business and seems to have few personal friends. The combination is ill-suited to her line of work, he thinks, but he's never brought it up. He doesn't know that she will be sensitive about it; the possibility is enough to scare him off. She, on her part, never speaks of her work, though they've known each other for six months. She has never expressed an opinion about his films.

She likes music, she loves to dance. She likes going to the movies.

So does he, like everyone else on this planet.

These are the things they talk about before they really get talking.

Like most people, they are almost normal.

They are close to each other, the two of them. Close as people can be that talk to each other on the phone incessantly. Their relationship, like themselves, is almost normal.

They have never met.

1.2

"Wrong numbers can be so serendipitous, don't you think?", she asks him, late one night.

"How so?", he replies.

"Well, if you hadn't called me by mistake, and you hadn't asked for someone I knew, and if I had known the number offhand, we would never have gotten to know each other. You know?"

"Right."

"Tell me something. Aren't you curious about me?"

"What do you mean?"

"You know. The way I look."

"Of course I am. You know that."

"Then why can't you just ask that person, the one we both know, the one you wanted to speak to when you ended up speaking with me?"

"Why don't you?"

"Maybe I'm not curious."

"Yes, and maybe you don't want me either."

"You know that's not true."

"I know," he says.

1.3

This is a conversation they're both used to having. Their responses have been perfected with practice: they catch each other out if an inflection is out of place. Sometimes, they spend an hour discussing an inflection. She tells him he needs to be honest with her: in a moment of honesty, he tells her that he can't afford to waste voice modulation on a woman he's never met. She doesn't call him back the next day. He waits and waits, and doesn't go to the gym, even though it shouldn't matter since his cellphone is charged and he doesn't ever miss paying his bills.

That night, he calls her.

1.4

"You know me very well. You know I care about these things."

"I know. I'm sorry."

"You can't be flippant about everything. Some things are serious. You know that."

"I do know that. I am sorry," he says.

"Don't do it again," she says. He thinks he can hear a sniff in her voice, but it could be his imagination. He doesn't bring it up.

"So. Friends again?", he asks eagerly.

"Yes."

She pauses, to collect herself, he feels, so he keeps quiet.

"How was your day?", she asks him then.

1.5

"This is very safe," he told her one day, many months ago, in the beginning of their relationship, in the safety and anonymity of the middle of a working day. The time, the setting, the thought that they were both in their offices and immersed in the minutiae of their working lives, all conspired to make their midday conversations trivial, like everyone else's. Not that day, however. That day, he was angry.

The uniform triviality of the workday call gave his voice an edge. I don't even know this woman, he had thought to himself as he dialed her number. I don't know what she looks like. I don't know what breed her dog is, I don't know what she ate this morning. What am I doing calling her now? Couples, married people, husbands and lovers: they call their partners at their offices, to ask them about their days, their plans, their thoughts about the cook's misadventures. Men like him, men of experience and advancing

years, didn't waste time calling women they hadn't met in the middle of the working day. It isn't in the rightness of things, it isn't
appropriate. It is adolescent, and finally, too fucking mundane. I
am not mundane, he had thought, as he punched in her number.
And he spoke to her of safety, with an edge in his voice.

"Aren't you a little bit bored?", he asked her. She stayed silent.
Not because she was bored, but because she didn't like the question. The area she worked in, spontaneous answers to difficult
questions weren't valued highly. So she listened to him, and hoped
that he would wind himself down. Before he did them both an
injury.

He had never been like this before, they both knew. He had
been petulant before, sometimes anxious. Always, he had wanted
more. But then, so did she, and the knowledge of their need being
mutual had kept him honest. But now, he was angry. Anger solved
nothing, she believed, and created many problems. He believed
the same thing, in truth, yet was powerless to unanger himself.

He carried on, the edge in his voice increasing. It teetered on
the edge of a shout, his voice, the only thing keeping it down the
tension in his throat as he mouthed words he wanted to scream.
Safety. Meeting. Needing. Communion. Words he couldn't see
coming to fruition in his own life.

"I want you too," she said finally. She said it, she thought,
because she wanted to calm him down. But as she said it, she knew
that she believed it.

"Then why don't you meet me?", he said, his voice almost
inaudible.

"Because I'm scared."

"Of what?"

"Infection."

The word hung there. It poisoned the air between them for a week, a week in which they didn't talk and waited for the other one to ring, to say that things hadn't changed. Finally, she called him. She asked him if anything had changed.

"No."

1.6

He has never been married. He has a child, he is reasonably sure, but he has never been asked by the mother to provide any sort of support: she doesn't even speak to him, and hasn't in several years. He has given up hoping that she will call: invite him to a PTA meeting, a birthday party perhaps. He has had a succession of pets, mostly two-legged, sometimes on all fours. He tried keeping goldfish once, and they died, one by one. He is too smart to have taken this as a sign. Yet, it is a fact that he has not had a pet since. Not on a leash, not in a skirt.

She was married, and isn't now. It isn't something she discusses at work. Her colleagues don't even know his name. There is a rumour that it was messy; sympathy was offered, when she came to the company. It was refused. She doesn't seem to have a mother that calls her at work, a father that sends her tickets home. Sometimes, when someone calls her at home for some work-related stuff, a dog can be heard barking somewhere in the background. In a house that none of her colleagues have ever been in. The occasional sound of the dog and the memory of his existence helps her co-workers deal with her. Still, there are occasional murmurings, and she seldom joins them for a drink after work. These days, they don't even ask. Mostly everyone thinks the end of her marriage was her own fault. If they knew that she loves dancing, they might think differently of her.

1.7

"I wish you were here right now," she says to him, while she lies on her bed in her home. Her voice is compressed, made husky in the way voices are when their owners are lying down and speaking on the phone.

He thinks he can imagine her lying there, perhaps playing with her hair with her free hand.

"I wish I was there too," he says in turn. He almost sighs it, but he would never admit to that. A man who is old enough to be balding; a filmmaker of his experience, in his view, shouldn't be sighing over the phone to a woman he has never met. But he almost does.

"Just think, all the things we could do," she says. He imagines her hands, playing with her hair. She could be stringing beads, he knows, but he prefers to think otherwise.

"What kinds of things," he asks her hungrily.

"You know," she says, turning over in her bed, snuggling down into the little depression her weight has made over time. "I don't need to tell you, you've been with women before." She can be coy, he has found. In anyone else, he finds it annoying. For her, he makes excuses.

"Yes I have," he says, "But I still want to hear you say it."

"Say what?"

"What we could be doing."

They talk about the things they could be doing that night, every night. Safely.

1.8

Sometimes she feels that it is insufferable. A woman like her, not young anymore, but not old; she shouldn't have to wait the entire day for a man to call her. Every now and then she catches herself waiting for the phone to ring. When that happens, she picks up the phone and calls him. The way she sees it, she is being free.

Her freedom sometimes extends to four, even five calls a day.

Freedom makes the time go faster, she has heard. At her age, time accelerating shouldn't be a good thing, she tells him one night, with a laugh. But what can you do? People need diversions, people need to hear other people's voices. People need people to need them. She says all this to him most nights. She says it to herself. Sometimes, she thinks that the faster time goes, the more she has to say it to herself. As if it is a mantra that will protect her, like a seatbelt: perhaps, more appropriately, a verbal airbag, when the crash comes. The thought diverts her. It makes her laugh. It makes her want to tell him the things he wants to hear, the good things that they could be doing together. It makes her want the same things.

And she continues to talk, till the thought that too much freedom may not be good or wise makes her hang up again.

Leaving him, literally, with his dick in his hand.

1.9

"It's been six months now," he says to her one night, when the time hangs heavy on his hands and he can hear her moving on her bed so clearly, he wishes he could see it as well. And he thinks, fuck it, I like stroking it as much as the next man, but now, finally, I want to wake up next to the woman I've been thinking about all this time. And with his impetuosity and his filmmaker's tongue, he thinks he can finally swing it. Besides, he feels he's earned it, and its not like he wants a quick shag. She should know that. He respects her wishes, he just wishes she would respect his.

"Exactly six months."

"I know," she says.

"Isn't it time, now, that we met?"

"Do you really want to meet me?", she asks him. "After all this time?" He thinks he hears a wondering in her voice. He tries to keep the edge of not knowing out of his own voice.

"I think I'm ready."

"Are you," she says, and is silent, with the weight of what is now unavoidable. He waits for her to go on.

"Aren't you the man," she says then, and almost laughs. It isn't a happy sound. He can hear the clock ticking right next to his bed, he is so quiet. The seconds tick away.

"And how would we protect ourselves?", she asks him then, her voice flat with anger.

"The usual ways."

"What? A condom for when you fuck me? A dental dam for when I blow you? What about you? Will you wear one too, when you go down on me? Well, will you? Or have you been lying to me all this time, about wanting to stick your face in my cunt?"

Mouths can get dry very quickly, he discovers, as he lies there on his bed, his ageing hand lying limply on his forgotten cock.

"Well? What do you intend to do? Only kiss and cuddle? Make spoons? Write numbers with our fingers on each other's backs, and change the sheets immediately after? How will you protect yourself? How will you protect me?"

And then they are both silent.

"What is wrong with you," he says finally.

"What do you mean," she replies.

Even tongues can get dry, in times of illness, and moments of stress. They can be powerless to wet lips that need it sorely. Yet he runs his bone-dry tongue around his lips in a futile attempt at moisture he knows he won't get over the phone. Not from her lips.

"What can I give you, you mad bitch, that you don't already have? What could you possibly give me?"

"That's what I'm afraid of," she replies, finally, and he catches the tenderness in her voice, and the questing.

"Oh," he says, guileless at last. And he stretches up towards the ceiling, up towards the sky, and he keeps the phone glued to his ear so that he can hear, away across the city, alone on her bed, a stranger of six month's standing breathe silently into her phone. And he remembers the tenderness, and he remembers the questing, and his own lack of pets these days.

So he says, "you know what I want to do to you right now?"

"What?", she says sleepily, the anger gone from her voice, and she settles herself more comfortably into her bed, in the little space the weight of her body has created in her mattress.

If her colleagues could see her right now, perhaps they wouldn't avoid her as they do, as if she were infected.

ANITA ROY

Harold and Me

"Perchance it might be properly said, there be three times:
a present of things past, a present of things present,
and a present of things future."—Confessions of St Augustine

TRYING to remember and reconstruct my meetings with Harold
Brodkey is a little like dragging a shadowy figure out of its corner
into the daylight. The steady, clear light which floods the *now*: the
present of things past, present and, maybe, future. In his treatise
on the mnemonic arts, Matteo Ricci—a 16th century Jesuit priest
—describes in great detail how to construct memory palaces:
architectural spaces held in the mind, where one places, with
great care and precision, figures whose posture and personality
enable us to recall past events, or information. The rooms of the
palace, he says, should be uncluttered and spacious; the light clear
and even, though not bright enough to dazzle; and the spaces
themselves must be clean and dry "lest the images be streaked

with rain or dew."

In constructing the memory palace where Brodkey lives in me, I have tried to keep these rules in mind. But the image of Brodkey himself, like the silhouette of a key, unlocks a flood of other messy and unruly sentiments which dazzle, streak, and clutter, refusing to stay in order. And memory itself emerges as less of a tool than the thing itself, not the chisel but the sculpture.

Brodkey's first claim to fame was that it took him nigh on thirty years to publish his first novel, *The Runaway Soul.* His first critically acclaimed collection of short stories, *First Love and Other Sorrows,* appeared in 1957. The American literary cognoscenti spent the next three decades waiting for The Novel, by turns gleeful and scornful, praising and denouncing him in roughly equal measure.

His second claim to fame was that he died of AIDS. His physical decline and his ferocious battle against disease were documented with characteristic unflinching self-regard in *This Wild Darkness,* published a few months after he died in 1996.

And his third claim to fame, not unrelated—in fact, intimately connected—to these first two, was what he calls "the myth of my *irresistibility:* The Fuck You Dreamed Of, Maybe." If Brodkey himself is to be believed, half of New York has been love with him at one time or another. He allies himself with Brando, Tennessee Williams and other such "sexy, bankrupt, Christ-like orphans". The devil in John Updike's book, *Witches of Eastwick,* played by Jack Nicholson in the film, was supposedly modeled on Brodkey. There was definitely something of the fallen angel about him. "It was an insiderish thing to be 'in love' with me," he recalls, "I cannot find in my memory a day in my life without some erotic drama or other."

And my claim to Brodkey? Nothing much—two brief encounters: that's it really. That and an extreme, unreasonably personal relationship to his books. Well, that one book actually: the runaway soul, kicking and bucking like an unbroken horse on the Illinois plains of his childhood, blistering the palms with its twisted reins.

The effort of memory required to reconstruct this patchy tale has been considerable, for one so careless and forgetful as me. It's a half-assed story, not quite satisfactory, though there are crowd-pleasing quasi-romantic moments and a tragic death to round things off. So, if you'll forgive the confessional tone—and I guess since we started with St Augustine, it's already somewhat excused —this rambling journal is an attempt to make amends, and recall what I can of the story.

✧

November 1991, Manchester UK

In the early '90s, I was working as a commissioning editor of academic books at Manchester University Press, and Waterstones bookshop on Deansgate was a regular haunt of mine. I loved the plush carpet, the well-stocked bookshelves and that quiet, self-absorbed bustle that good bookshops seem to specialise in. *The Runaway Soul* had just been published and reviewers had gone to town on it—although they wrote less about the book itself than about its author.

"Harold Brodkey is about to become America's greatest writer," pronounced *The Guardian* in July that year, "That's what they say in New York, and it's what they've been saying ever since his first, extraordinary stories were published more than 30 years ago. But Brodkey is still widely unknown, and his first novel, decades in the making, is still being edited. 'Either I am truly great,' he says, 'or I am a fraud.'" The publication of his magnum opus had already been announced, prematurely, at least twice—in the *New York Times* in 1977, and then again in the *Washington Post* in 1986. It had finally appeared and I was amazed and a bit taken aback that the author himself would be doing a reading at Waterstones.

I bicycled through the perennial Manchester drizzle to the bookshop, propped my bike outside, and joined the throng, seated in rows in front of a small desk piled high with copies of the book. The first word that came into my mind seeing Brodkey in the flesh, was 'dapper'. His salt-and-pepper beard was trimmed as neatly and to the exact same length as his hair. He surveyed the room with piercingly intelligent, mischievous black eyes. Dressed in a dark turtle-neck sweater and a tweedy jacket, he was the picture of elegance: very Conneryesque. There was something trim, yet muscular about him, pared-down but tough, like he worked out a lot. You just knew that if he smoked, he'd smoke really, *really* well—thoughtfully, intensely, and with a great deal of style. His wife, Ellen Schwamm, was there at his side looking twinkly and slightly nervous. She had a quick, engaging smile.

After the bookshop manager's reverential intro, Brodkey started to read: "I was slapped and hurried along in the private applause of birth—I think I remember this well." The opening line of *The Runaway Soul*. Of course he would start with the narrator recalling his own birth—where else would you start to tell the story of your own life?

> " —the blind boy's rose-and-milk and gray-walled (and salty) aquarium, the aquarium overthrown, the uproar in the woman-barn ... the fantastic sloppiness of one's com ing into existence, one's early election, one's sense in the radiant and raw stuff of howlingly sore and unexplained registry in the new everywhere..."

By the time he got to the phrase "the awful contamination of actual light", I was hooked, line and sinker. Now *this,* I thought to myself, is a *writer*. He read rather well, with a kind of amused substrate that tinted the actual, audible words like a strong-colour undercoat on a freshly painted wall.

He fielded questions from the audience with immense courtesy, and finally the evening drew to a close in a flurry of book-signing. I bought my copy, and procrastinated until the very end of the line when, I'd hoped, as his pen hovered over the page, names would be exchanged... and possibly phone numbers... and then, who knows? I don't remember and can't reconstruct our conversation. I said something cheeky and cutting which sort of got his attention and made him laugh, and we traded insults for a while which was nice.

He wrote diagonally across the whole title page of the book, in big, bold biro: "November 1991. For Anita Roy—with memories of Manchester, England. Harold Brodkey."

I carefully stashed the book in my bag, water-proofed against the rain outside, and cycled away through the dark, reflective streets, zigzagging a little, like I was drunk, or in love.

✣

I remember the next few weeks reading the novel. I would lie on my front, resting on my elbows with my head propped up with my hands—it was the only position I found could comfortably accommodate the size and weight of the thing. It was the physical demand the book made.

I found myself going really, really slowly. Sometimes I'd catch myself just looking at the page, like a bewildered typesetter. What I hadn't realised, and what could not be conveyed from listening to him read, was how utterly and furiously weird he is about punctuation. Each page was littered with ellipses and colons, sudden outbursts of italics, whole phrases linked together with dashes and then casually made into an adverb; attention-grabbing small caps; commas and full-stops used more like a choreographer might use gesture than a linguist to convey sense. Christ, I remember thinking, this must have been a *nightmare* to copyedit. He is the jazz master of punctuation, doing unto grammar as Charlie Parker does unto melody. Wringing from every sentence its last ounce of elusive nuance, but with this dramatic artlessness—a kind of wide-gestured innocence and blunder. His writing seemed fantastically uncontrolled—a real runaway, an unbroken horse, a driverless locomotive.

I seemed to spend forever reading the book. It wasn't just that the punctuation was odd. It was that the obsessiveness with which he tracked down, and dissected to its minutest part each individual moment of feeling, demanded an almost equally obsessive attention on the part of his reader. In a piece for *The Guardian* in July 1991, James Wood wrote that the "real originality [of Brodkey's work] lies in its relationship to meaning. Brodkey believes he is the first writer to search at the deepest level of meaning, to explore the intimacies of consciousness. ... Brodkey sinks language down into meaning, revealing previous writers as mere skimmers of truth. His writing has a mad focus. He scours meaning for its gradations and minute privacies. He searches it out, touches its tenderest places... At the deepest level, Brodkey's writing is attempting to capture the passage of time, individual seconds and moments caught in such fullness and attention that one no longer thinks of time as consecutive (a progress), but as jagged, layered, exhaustingly diffuse." The present, in other words, of things past.

Reading *The Runaway Soul* was like being forced to re-live an entire life—in this case, that of Wiley Silenowicz, adopted Jewish Midwestern boy (none of which, co-incidentally, I am). It was the most extraordinary sensation. It was as though Wiley's memories, written out so relentlessly, actually became my own. This was more than mere 'identification'; I felt like I'd been rigged up to one of those infernal machines you get in 1950 sci-fi movies, with trailing wires from a metal helmet linking one person to another and performing some kind of brain-transfer.

The difference between life and fiction is that life rarely makes sense, it is incoherent and rambling and full of randomness and incidental characters and insignificant coincidence. Fiction sifts out the meaninglessness and chaos of lived reality and imposes a coherence—even if of an altogether loose and seemingly chaotic type—on the whole godawful mess.

Memory, some might say, is our attempt to impose a retrospective order on things past—to tell ourselves the *story*. Humans are notoriously bad at remembering—we edit, cut and paste, repress, dismiss, and simplify. Brodkey, unlike the rest of us skimmers of truth, seems blessed—or cursed—with total recall. And *The Runaway Soul,* unlike any other novel I've ever read, brings that to the page with a startling immediacy. He absolutely *refuses* to approximate. Even the most fleeting and inchoate hint of a sensation is captured in his wild net of language.

"Brodkey," writes Wood, "wants to capture the *amateurishness* of our lives—every clumsy sensation." And every clumsy memory too. Reading Harold Brodkey's prose is both like *having a* memory —that slipshod, grasping, half-incoherent struggle to recollect—and like *living through* an actual experience, though the experience may simply be that of having the memory. That might sound like you're receding from reality, at one too many removes of separation, but it's actually not. Reading Brodkey one has the eerie sensation of eavesdropping on another person's thought patterns—being, for the duration of the page, or the sentence, or the chapter, inside *their head* looking out or, for that matter, looking in.

It's as though the language is constantly rushing at reality, grasping at and ricocheting off the real. One chapter in the novel describes Wiley, as a young boy, after the death of his father. He bicycles off to the river, wades in, pisses and then masturbates into water, turns round and goes home. Mundane moments—yet recalled with such a complete sense of the intersecting eddies of thought and reality that the reader is transported—almost transposed—into the mind and body of that mortal fragment of adolescent bravery and grief.

"I tied the dinghy to a log, half-buried in the mud. And I climbed out of the boat into the muddy water; I feel my lower legs moistly muddied in the water ... my bare feet are in the gooey mud of the bottom ... river molluscs cut my feet and the river shrimp tickle my ankles. My feet and lower legs are as if murmuring with sensation. My gym shoes, their laces tied, are around my neck. The quick pulsations of fear and the alternating and, maybe, ruling bravery, or recklessness, and the thing of how it felt to be really alone for a change, the expansion of the mind then—as if your own mind became a mother or a brother there with you for the day, going along with you for the day's stuff—and to be alone in this wobbly state of bravery with no audience, I had come here for this but hadn't really remembered from before what it was really like..."

It's like the poet John Ashbery wrote in 'The Ice-Cream Wars':

Although I mean it, and project the meaning
As hard as I can into its brushed-metal surface,
It cannot, in this deteriorating climate, pick up
Where I leave off.

The physicality of stuff, of objects, of things, always seems in excess of our attempts to make sense of them. Brodkey, however, comes much closer than most to making meaning stick.

Wiley's life shares many similarities to Brodkey's own.

Brodkey's own mother died when he was a toddler, and he, like Wiley, was adopted, as a young kid, by a mid-Western Jewish couple. His adoptive father sexually abused him as a child, and died when Brodkey was twelve years old. Who knows what other incidents in the book 'actually happened'—they all, without exception, crackle with authenticity.

When I finally finished the book, I wrote to Brodkey. He'd told me, half-joking, at the reading, that I should write and let him know what I thought of it. And I'd responded with something flirtatiously crass like "What, even if I think it's crap?" And he'd laughed and said, "Yeah, even then." So I did. I cannot remember what I said: I'm sure it was a gush of sub-Brodkeyian blah, but I was still reeling from the book, the brain-wires connecting me and Wiley hadn't yet finished humming, and I was still woozy from the experience. It's a strange thing, writing to an author of a book you've admired. I'd never done it before. As a reader, you feel that you *know* this person, that, through the experience of the book, you've already *had* a fairly long and intimate relationship, and that continuing this into the real light of day, should present no problem. But to the writer, you're... well, what? No one, right? Just another anonymous face in the crowd. Anyway, I sent off the letter to Brodkey, care of *The New Yorker* magazine with a what-have-I-got-to-lose shrug and expected nothing further.

About a month later, a small white envelope turned up on my desk at work, containing two sheets of notepad paper. He had written back. Somewhere in a box in my parent's attic there is this letter. I've kept it somewhere so safely that I can't remember where it is. He thanked me for my letter, and said how much it meant to him that a reader—rather than these fuck-all critics (about whom he was notoriously dismissive)—should respond to his work. He described the spring happening outside his window. His handwriting was neat and fluent. He ended by saying if I ever happened to be in New York, here was his number.

September 1992, New York

I had been sent to New York for a series of meetings with our American co-publishers. The offices of St Martin's Press were located in the wedge of the flatiron building in Manhattan. The ritzy appeal of being a young professional woman, striding purposefully down 5th Avenue with a styrofoam beaker of cappuccino in one hand and a satchel of contracts over my shoulder was not lost on me. The building keeled into view, as incongruous and regal as a luxury liner run aground in the middle of the city. Its outer grandeur belied the cramped and angular interior, where the cabins on either side of the narrow corridor got more and more triangular until I reached the office of the head of academic publishing exactly in the prow. Between the strange angularity, the cramped quarters and the heaps of papers lying around, it felt a little like hiding out in the cupboard under the stairs.

I had called Harold from my hotel room the same evening as I'd arrived. I had no idea if he would remember me, or if he did, what he would say, but the just-the-two-of-us *intimacy* of his handwritten letter steeled my resolve, and I dialed the number.

"Hello?" A woman's voice answered in carefully modulated tones.

"Er, hello," I said, "Could I speak to Harold Brodkey?"

"Sure, I'll see if he's free."

There was a pause, then Harold picked up the phone.

"Hello, I don't know if you remember me, but umm, this is Anita, Anita Roy? From Manchester? I've just arrived in New York and you'd said if I was ever…"

"Oh hi! Anita!" He sounded sort of pleased and puzzled, but mostly pleased. I heaved a sigh of relief. "Can you just hold for a second, there's someone on the other line."

I was put on hold by Harold Brodkey. The mere thought gave me a subcutaneous thrill that stood my hairs on end. He came back on line, asking how long I'd be here and if we could meet up.

"That would be wonderful," I said. "When?"

We fixed to have lunch together on Friday and he gave me the address of a macrobiotic restaurant downtown. I put the receiver back on the cradle, and fell backwards on to the bed, giggly with relief.

One of the main reasons for me being in New York was to try and fix a co-pub deal on a book which I'd signed up and was then in production. I was convinced then, and remain so, that it was one of the most important academic works to be published, and the thrill I got daily from knowing that I was midwifing this extraordinary book into the world, added to my sense of elation. Written by Elisabeth Bronfen, unquestionably the most intelligent and well-read women I'd ever met, it linked together death and femininity, art and culture, from Abelard and Helouise to Diane Arbus and Marilyn Monroe. I was passionately convinced of the importance of this work, which made promoting it—and the author—a doddle. My evangelical zeal paid off, and the deal was in the bag.

That Thursday, I made my way to the headquarters of Condé Nast, there to meet the grand old man of Vogue himself, Leo Lerman. The offices on Madison Avenue oozed an understated class, elegance and style. As I was escorted to Mr Lerman's inner sanctum by his personable young assistant, I strived to carry myself with the insouciance of the Arrived. The décor was that of a sought-after gentleman's club, with original lithographs framed on oak-paneled walls. I stood to attention, fighting the urge to clean my shoes on the backs of my trousers, and feeling hopelessly out of my depth. Mr Lerman was graciousness itself, and listened to my ravings about death and culture with a seriousness for which I felt almost tearfully grateful. He agreed to try and carry an article on this brilliant new academic author in one or other of his magazines. I mentioned that I would be meeting Harold Brodkey the following day—I can't now remember *why* or how that would have been relevant to our conversation; I probably just blurted it out in an effort to appear more well-connected and sophisticated and, well, *Jewish*, than I was. Mr Lerman raised a grizzled eyebrow in polite interest, and delivered me again unto Stephen, the charming P.A., who ushered me out.

Friday morning's meeting went by in a blur, and I was kind of twittery with nervousness by lunchtime. It suddenly seemed like a terrible idea. Why on earth was I meeting this guy? Did I suppose this was the beginning of a beautiful relationship? Could we possibly be *friends*? I mean, come on. Get real. I didn't even have a vaguely professional excuse to meet him as I had with Mr Lerman. I had nothing to show him, or give him, or anything. I almost bolted.

I found the restaurant and sat, facing the door. When Brodkey came in, I was startled. He seemed to have aged ten years from the dapper raconteur that I'd met less than a year previously. The creases bracketing his mouth had become deeper and more dragged down. He'd gone from trim to gaunt. I put this down to my own bad memory of how he had looked, and soldiered on through what was an increasingly stilted and pointless conversation. I think he thought that I was someone else; and neither of us could quite work out what we were doing there. The food was simple and healthful, but I couldn't wait for it to be done with. I felt like an impostor. I felt like I'd somehow let the side down.

Watching him walk away down the street, he looked like an unremarkable old man. I felt like running after him and apologising. I don't know what got into me. I just stood there, dumbly, in the benediction of light on that Fall afternoon, watching him leave, and feeling like an utter fool.

✛

June 1993, Manchester
Sunday morning in my flat in Manchester. My boyfriend tosses the paper to me, saying "Hey, isn't this that guy that you liked so much?" and there it is. A full page picture of him looking quizzical and grizzled and a bit contemptuous, a heavy-gilt framed oil painting slightly out of focus behind. The piece is entitled: 'To My Readers' and begins: "I have AIDS." I couldn't read beyond the second sentence for crying. Of course he was ill when I saw him. I cannot imagine what it cost him to get up, go out, and walk to the restaurant for what turned out to be an entirely pointless rendezvous with some woman who he thought was someone else. A fresh surge of pointless remorse swept through me. It seemed so

obvious in retrospect. It was not my faulty memory of what he had looked like the year before. It was my incredible obtuseness in not recognising, even when it was before me plain as day, that here was a man seriously ill, possibly dying. I felt so fucking *stupid*.

Towards the end of the essay, he wrote:

> "Not constantly but not inconstantly either, underneath the sentimentality and obstinacy of my attitudes are, as you might expect, a quite severe rage and a vast, a truly extensive terror, anchored in contempt for you and for life and for everything. But let's keep that beast in its gulf of darkness. Let's be polite and proper and devoted to life now as we were earlier in our life on this planet."

And I was reminded again of Ashbery's poem, which ends:

> 'the truth becomes a hole, something one has always known,
> A heaviness in the trees, and no one can say
> Where it comes from, or how long it will stay
> A randomness, a darkness of one's own.'

The random darkness of Brodkey's dying was his and his alone.

I nevertheless felt impelled to make one last attempt at connection—a bit futile, a bit *late in the day* you might say, but anyway. I sent off a letter to Harold expressing I don't know what—grief, solidarity, an apology, a farewell—what do you tell a man who's dying?

Sixteen months later, at the end of October 1994, another little New Yorker envelope arrived on my desk at work, this time from his wife. This is what she wrote:

> Dear Anita
> An absurd thing happened to us. We spent a month in
> Venice last August and asked the New Yorker to hold our
> mail until our return. It was only two days ago that a huge
> packet arrived from the New Yorker with apologies. They
> had never resumed forwarding the mail and would prob
> ably have kept it forever but it had begun to take over the
> mailroom. Your sweet letter was among the few that
> Harold wanted me to answer immediately.
> We are… glad to hear from you. Harold does have some
> good days but mostly it's a matter of good minutes or even
> good mornings, if he's lucky. He is working through it all
> and printing regularly in the New Yorker. He sends his
> best. And I send mine.
> Sincerely,
> Ellen

✣

January 1996, London

When I read in the newspaper that he'd died, I breathed a sigh of
relief. Though he said, in his 'To My Readers' address, "I don't
want to talk about my dying to everyone, or over and over", this is
precisely what he did. The 'working through it all' described by
Ellen resulted in a small book, published a few months after he
died, entitled *This Wild Darkness: The Story of my Death.*

Brushes with death were nothing new for Brodkey. With the unconscious perversity of one who never did things by halves, his infrequent illnesses were almost always almost fatal. Faced with the inevitable, he set about dissecting his own physical decline, and attendant emotions in minute detail.

> "If you train yourself as a writer to look at these things—
> this vulnerability, when the balance is gone and the
> defenses are undone so that you are open to viruses and
> their shocking haywire excitement—then facing them
> becomes almost habitual. You will have the real material,
> and it will arise from this new-to-you dense memory of
> being jostled by medical and natural violence to the edge
> of life."

Don DeLillo, to whom many have passed the mantle of 'America's Greatest Living Writer' (now that Brodkey is dead), described Brodkey's progress as a writer as "one of the great brave journeys of American literature." Brodkey's Moby Dick, which he pursued throughout his life with such fixity of purpose and Ahab-like disregard, was that many-headed hydra of memory and reality —how to capture memories in language, how to work the language until it became sufficiently rich and nuanced that not a single fragment of meaning could slip its fine mesh, how to write *life* in all its bewildering, chaotic diversity.

> "God as a term for all of whatever reality there is—the
> universe, all the universes—God as a term used by my
> soul seems to signal that *He* loves the present tense even

more than consciousness does … Our sense of present
ness usually proceeds in waves, with our minds tumbling
off into wandering. Usually, we return and ride the wave
and tumble and resume the ride and tumble, and in the
act of tumbling we are ourselves, egocentrically, and
things are seen and known to us. *Actual reality may
belong to the present tense, but this falling away and
return is what we are.*[his italics]"

Towards the end of his life he wrote: "Today I cannot find anything in my life to be proud of—love or courage or acts of generosity. Or my writing. My life has been mostly error. Error and crap."
Then, on the same page, he remembers, and captures the memory in writing, the wild light of writing against the wild darkness of
approaching death:

"I remember Chartres in 1949 before the stained glass
was restored. No one I had spoken to and nothing I'd
read had prepared me for the delicacy of the colours, the
pale blue, a sky blue really, and the yellow. The transcen
dent theatre of the nave while the light outside changed
moment to moment—clouds blowing over—and the
colours brightening or darkening in revolving whorls
inside the long, slanted beams of lady-light. I had never
been *inside* a work of genius before."

✣

October 1996, New Delhi

An American friend sent me a story from *The New Yorker* written by Brodkey in the last months of his life. The main characters from *The Runaway Soul*, Wiley and his lover Ora, take a tumble in the hay—well, in the moonlit grass—in 'Dumbness is Everything'. It is without doubt some of the best sex that has ever made it to the page. The interiority of it, that thing of being joined and utterly separate, the closeness and the isolation, the constant inner dialogue and the brief fall-from-paradise silence when it is overwhelmed by physical sensation:

> "Ora's body is a landscape, a climate—or a kind of boat—
> for my feelings. She doesn't dance or wriggle or seduce
> with her body. There is some huge gulf between her body
> as visible and affecting you and its inward or private reali
> ty for her as heat; and that divergence is what you touch."

It is the story of the stories that we tell ourselves when we have sex. It has narrative drive. "Drunkenly, I saw the usefulness of disliking her kiss; its usefulness as a plot device; it goaded me to roll on top of her, a little more down the slope, on the tickling, faintly harsh grass. I want to control the sloppiness of her kiss, turn it into sensual coherence." It is the tumbling surf of life-as-fiction and fiction-as-life, the alternate waves of tumbling away from and towards reality that make up our every moment, that tells us who we *are*. "To propose reality as a story rather than a story as reality might at least remind you what a prior thing experience is. And how we hide it in stories."

For anyone to write about sex with this intense *interest* is an extraordinarily affirmative act. For someone staring at death, whose body had been riddled by disease and pumped full of drugs, it is almost the definition of hubris. Just take a look at the nouns in the title of his last (post-humous) collection of stories: *The World is the Home of Love and Death.* How the hell could one *not* fall in love with him?

November 2000, New Delhi

As well as the mnemonic art of building memory palaces, Matteo Ricci was fascinated by the power of symbols—Chinese ideograms, as well as the written word—the almost heretical power of human marks on the page to transcend time as well as space:

> "Those who will live one hundred generations after us are not yet born, and I cannot tell what sort of people they will be. Yet thanks to the existence of written culture even those living ten thousand generations hence will be able to enter into my mind as if we were contemporaries. As for those worthy figures who lived a hundred generations ago, although they too are gone, yet thanks to the books they left behind we who come after can hear their modes of discourse, observe their grand demeanor, and under stand both the good order and the chaos of their times, exactly as if we were living among them."

The diary entries, scraps of newspaper, letters, and notes, no less than Brodkey's books themselves, are mnemonic talismans recalling him to my mind. The present of things past twining its fingers around those of the present of things present. A hand-holding that is mysteriously healing.

Objectivity is second only to chastity in being the most overrated virtue. How is it possible to lean back and coolly view a loved one's face with a scientific eye—and why on earth would you want to? So, on second thoughts, I won't apologise for this highly subjective essay. Someone who fell in love with me once described our first meeting as being like in a novel when you know that the other main character has just turned up. I felt something like that about Harold Brodkey. Reading him evokes a younger being than I am now, who used to go at the world with a deeper, or perhaps just more reckless, give-away attack and joy. Remembering him recalls her, and I miss that person that I used to be, even as I mock and regret her idiocies. Perhaps both reading and remembering are a reminder that the urge to make fiction out of our lives is nothing less than the struggle to wrest meaning from its daily randomness: an adventure, a grand quest and even, at times and for some brave or runaway souls, a heroic one.

URVASHI BUTALIA

The Persistence
of Memory

ON 11 MARCH 1947, Sant Raja Singh of Thoa Khalsa village in
Rawalpindi district, picked up his sword, said a short prayer to
Guru Nanak, and then, with one swift stroke, brought it down on
the neck of his young daughter, Maan Kaur. As the story is told, at
first he didn't succeed; the blow wasn't strong enough...something
came in the way. Then his daughter, aged sixteen, came once again
and knelt before her father, removed her thick plait, and offered
him her neck. This time, his sword found its mark. Bir Bahadur
Singh, his son of eleven, stood by his side and watched. Years later,
he recounted this story to me: 'I stood there, right next to him,
clutching on to his kurta as children do... I was clinging to him,
sobbing, and her head rolled off and fell... there... far away.'

Shortly after this incident, Bir Bahadur's family fled Thoa
Khalsa, heading towards the Indian border where they hoped to
find safety. India was being partitioned, and large-scale carnage,
arson, rape and loot among Muslims, Hindus and Sikhs had

become the order of the day. In many families, like Bir Bahadur's, the men decided to kill women and children, fearing that they would be abducted, raped, converted, impregnated, polluted by men of the other religion—in this case Muslims. They called these killings the 'martyrdom of women'.

It was only two years earlier, in 1945, that Bir Bahadur's family had moved to Thoa Khalsa. Talk of a possible partition was in the air and they were worried for their safety. Saintha, the village in which they had lived for many years was a Muslim majority village and theirs was the only non-Muslim family there. It was this that made Bir Bahadur's father, Sant Raja Singh, decide to move to Thoa Khalsa, where there were many more Sikhs than Muslims. Everywhere, at this time, people banded together with their own kind, believing that safety lay in numbers. Ironically, and tragically, it was in Thoa Khalsa that the real violence took place. In retaliation for attacks by Hindus and Sikhs on Muslims elsewhere in India, villages in this part of Rawalpindi—inhabited mainly by Sikhs—came under concerted attack for several days.

Forty years later, Bir Bahadur told me these stories. I had met him while researching a book on oral histories of the Partition of India. In the lower middle class area of Delhi where he lived, Bir Bahadur was someone people looked up to—he came from a family of martyrs. Not only his sister, but several other women had been killed on that day. Bir Bahadur had been a young boy at the time, but his memories of the time were crystal clear and sharp. He remembered the fear and the violence and remembered too that when the attacks had begun to seem imminent, people from his 'home' village of Saintha had come to Thoa in a delegation to offer his family protection in Saintha. They were led by Sajawal Khan, the village headman. But his father had turned them away. They were Muslims and, although he had lived among them in safety and peace for many years, he no longer trusted them. Bir Bahadur has never forgotten this rejection.

Stories of such violence—and more—are routine when Muslims and Hindus speak of the Partition of the Indian subcontinent in 1947. The British decision to partition the country into two, India and Pakistan, led to the displacement of millions of people, a million deaths, and nearly a hundred thousand incidents of rape and abduction. Many other forms of violence became commonplace. Women were particularly vulnerable: not only was there mass rape and abduction but hundreds were killed by their own families, ostensibly as a form of 'protection', some had their breasts cut off, others had symbols of the 'other' religion tattooed on their bodies. But while stories of violence are routine, what is less known are the stories of friendship that cut across the rigid borders drawn by the Indian and Pakistani States. In the year 2000 Bir Bahadur and I embarked on one such journey of friendship and reconciliation across what had till then seemed like a somewhat intractable border.

It all began with a phone call from Chihiro, a Japanese journalist. She was keen to make a programme featuring an Indian travelling to Pakistan on the India-Pakistan bus, visiting his/her relatives. She, and a crew, would travel along with this person and film the journey as well as the 'homecoming'. She asked for suggestions. I offered Bir Bahadur's name. For years he had wanted to go back to his home village in Pakistan, but had never had the opportunity, [not because it is expensive but because visas between the two countries are almost impossible to get.] Now it had presented itself.

Now in his seventies, Bir Bahadur Singh is a tall, statuesque Sikh with a white flowing beard. Always dressed in white, with a black turban and a saffron headcloth showing through, he makes an arresting figure and stands out in a crowd. Bir Bahadur's family was only one among the millions of refugees who fled from Pakistan to India. They carried nothing with them and Bir Bahadur's key memories of that time are of hunger, fear and cold. Once in India, Bir Bahadur and his family struggled to keep body and soul together. He tried his hand at different things and then, at 18, he managed to put together enough to set up a small provision store. Later, his family arranged for him to marry a woman from a village close to his home in Rawalpindi, and together they brought up a large family. Bir Bahadur has never been rich, and he has worked hard all his life for the sake of his children. A might-have-been politician (he stood for municipal elections on a Bharatiya Janata Party ticket some years ago and lost) Bir Bahadur now leads a retired life, dividing his time between his farmhouse close to Delhi, his extended family of children and grandchildren, and his old (90 plus) mother who lives close by. He was beside himself with excitement at the news that he might get permission to travel to Pakistan and visit his home village.

With Japanese intervention visas were swiftly arranged and a few days later, we left for Pakistan. Bir Bahadur arrived at my house with a small bag and a sackful of hard, dry coconuts. These were to be his offerings to the people of his village. 'There are no coconuts there,' he explained, 'and people love to have them.' He had also written two letters, one to the people of his village, and one to his school friend, Sadq Khan, son of Sajawal Khan. 'We were good friends in school,' he said, 'I am sure he will remember me.' These he carried with him, in the event that we did not make it to the village. He was convinced we would find someone, somewhere, who would carry his letters to the village, and people from there would arrive in immediate response, to see him. For days he'd been like a child, excited and nervous. He'd rung me every day—sometimes twice or three times in a day—to check on this or that detail. Would we be staying in a hotel ? How much money should he bring ? Would I be with them the whole time ? Could we not persuade Chihiro to do a radio programme instead of one for television (we did)—it would be much less obvious. And now that we were actually on our way, he could not believe his luck.

Heavy rain and bad monsoon weather had delayed the flight. We spent a long and tiring night waiting at Lahore airport, uncomfortable in plastic seats. Occasionally, Chihiro and I would doze off out of sheer exhaustion. But not Bir Bahadur. Every time I opened my eyes, I found him wide awake, sitting on his haunches in the airport chairs, recounting his story to someone or the other—now a family on their way to Karachi (also delayed), now two helpful employees of the airline (with whom he was quickly exchanging photographs and addresses) and now the toyshop owner or the man selling tea... Hazy with sleep, I wondered wearily whether there was anyone at the airport he'd left out of this storytelling.

✥

Islamabad is a city of wide boulevards and tree-lined roads. At night, speeding through the deserted streets, there was little to see. We arrived, exhausted, at our hotel at 3 in the morning after a 12-hour delay in our flight. But this did not seem to have affected Bir Bahadur. Why did we want to wait till 10 to set off in the morning he asked plaintively, 'I won't be able to sleep, let's go at 6 !' But this proposal was shot down firmly by our Japanese friend, and the time of our departure fixed for 10.

The morning rose clean and washed. Heavy rain had cooled things down and the sun seemed almost mild, the air clear of the oppressive humidity of the monsoon, the trees and plants a rich, freshly-washed green. Armed with some water and our passports and visa papers, we set off for Thoa Khalsa. A wide, straight, road led through fairly flat terrain to the outskirts of Islamabad. We'd been driving for an hour or so when we arrived at a major turnoff. Clearly some sort of junction, the wide road was bordered at this point with small shops selling fruit, juices, cigarettes, food and snacks and all the small knicknacks that travellers buy when they make stopovers. On the other side was a bus and tempo terminal, with scooter and tempo drivers shouting out their locations, picking up point-to-point passengers and quickly shuffling men into separate seats the moment they saw prospective women passengers: one of the unwritten rules of tempo travelling in Pakistan (and indeed often in India too) is that men and women do not occupy the same seat lest they inadvertently touch each other. We stopped to ask directions and then, turned off onto a narrower road to the left. A gate across the road proclaimed a level crossing, and a small signpost gave the name of the station: Manolia. 'This used to be our station,' Bir Bahadur told me excitedly, 'the train stopped here, and we'd have to take buses from our village to get here !' We stopped in the marketplace to get a better look at the station. Immediately the car was surrounded by a crowd of people —tall, hefty men in shalvar kameezes. They were everywhere: at the doors, in front of the car, virtually inside the driver's door. We couldn't move, and I began to panic a bit. In such situations the enmity and rhetoric of hatred that India and Pakistan constantly rehearse comes back to haunt us, and, although the situation is harmless enough, it suddenly acquires overtones of fear. But Bir Bahadur was unfazed: 'Stop, stop the car,' he told the driver unnecessarily, and wound his window down. He leaned out, trained his gaze on the tea stall across the road and said, to no one in particular: 'Bhai sahib, bhai sahib, excuse me, can you help ?' A cyclist stopped by to see what it was he wanted, and the crowd of men surrounding the car suddenly transformed themselves from a threatening bunch to a group of curious and helpful onlookers peering into the car at two strange women, and an odd man, clearly from over the border for he had on a turban and there were no Sikhs in the area. 'Welcome, welcome, sardarji,' they said, 'where have you come from ? India ? What are you looking for here ? Can we help you to find it ?' Bir Bahadur immediately launched into his story while Chihiro and I sat nervously wondering if it was wise, in an unknown place in Pakistan, to recall stories of the violence of Partition.

'I'm from this area,' he told them, 'my father used to run a shop in Saintha, and I am looking for the road to Saintha. Do you know Sajawal Khan from Saintha ?'

'Not Saintha', I whispered to him, 'we need to know how to get to Thoa Khalsa.'

'Yes, yes,' he said, turning to the man, 'and we need to get to Thoa Khalsa as well. But first, I want to find Saintha.'

It was at this point that it became clear to me that Bir Bahadur had already decided on the itinerary for this trip—no matter that Chihiro wanted to capture the drama of taking him back to the place where he had seen such a bloody history, he was determined to go to Saintha, his home village. I felt a curious mixture of relief (that we may not now have to confront what could have been an unpleasant situation) and elation (that he had succeeded in doing exactly what he wanted) and concern (for Chihiro and her radio programme which, after all, had paid for us to be here). While these thoughts were turning around in my head and I was wondering how to break the news to Chihiro, I suddenly found that Bir Bahadur had invited one of the men outside into the car. Basheer, he told us, was a son-in-law of Saintha, and had offered to ride there with us and help us find the place and the people Bir Bahadur was looking for. 'Can you slide up a bit Beta ?' he said to me, and I pushed myself into as small a corner as I could, to make room for a rather large and hefty Basheer. We were breaking the unwritten code here: three of us in the backseat, one woman and two men. The available space was tight, and it was up to me to ensure that our bodies remained at least an inch apart. Meanwhile, everyone on the road offered us advice and suggestions for free, one person ran off and came back with six bananas, another asked if we'd like a cold drink, we must be tired, while a third offered us mithai. Finally, they waved us off with good wishes, extracting a promise from us that we would come back this way and stop for a cup of tea and some sweets.

And so we set off, down a long, straight road, past large fields, and scattered homes, the occasional tractor carrying bales of straw, groups of women drawing water at village wells, their faces partially veiled, and slowly the landscape gave way to a gentle, hilly terrain. We could have been in India: everything looked exactly as it would do on the other side of the border, in Punjab: the roadside shops, the villages with their mud houses, the scene at the well, the fields covered with stalks of wheat pushing their way out of the earth. 'Son,' said Bir Bahadur to Bahseer after a few minutes, 'just keep telling me the names of the places we are passing along the way, just keep reminding me.' Dutifully, Basheer did as he was told, and at one point, as we were passing a small rise on our left with a stray houses scattered along its slopes, bordered by stubby bushes on the road, Basheer said 'that village is called Thamali.'

'Stop, stop,' Bir Bahadur said to Sain, our driver, 'please stop, Thamali is where my wife used to live, it's her village.' We swung over to the side of the narrow road, and Bir Bahadur and Basheer leapt out of the car and began climbing. ' I can't believe it,' said Bir Bahadur excitedly, 'we used to come here to play. There, there's the banyan tree we used to sit under, and over that hill was her grandfather's house, the water pump—please,' he said, turning to me, 'please can you take a picture of me by the tree, I'd like to take it back to my wife.' As he stood there waiting to be photographed, the tree behind him, a small knot of people—husband, wife, perhaps a brother or brother-in-law and two children, came out of a nearby house. Bir Bahadur greeted the children, affectionately patting them on the head, and waited as the parents drew up. They came, faces open with welcome: 'where are you from

Sardarji, how have you come here ? Won't you come to our home and drink some sherbet with us ?'

'No, no my child,' said Bir Bahadur to the young woman, 'thank you for your welcome my daughter. This village Thamali is where my wife comes from. I used to play here as a child 50 years ago, long before you were even born. See, see that tree over there ? That was the tree we sat under. My wife's family home was over that hill, there was a pond and a water pump there...' The pond was still there they told him, but of course the water pump had gone. The school too—the building was there, but it was no longer used as a school. Thamali had been at the receiving end of the Muslim attack on Sikhs in March 1947 and large numbers of people had been killed. Looking at the small, peaceful village nestling in the July sun, it seemed hard to believe that such violence could have taken place there. I tried to picture the mobs everyone—not only Bir Bahadur—had told me about, the countryside resounding with the cries of murder and revenge, the thirst for blood. How would they have moved from village to village, I wondered inconsequentially, this thin ribbon of a road was probably not there at the time. How must people have felt to see hundreds, thousands of attackers coming over these gentle, almost sleepy, slopes? What protection did their houses offer? At which points did they negotiate? What do people do when violence breaks out in this way? The people of Thamali, I remembered being told, had refused to believe initially that they could be attacked. Then, someone from another village had persuaded them to climb atop one of the higher houses and look down at the area around them, and they'd done so and seen the mobs and quickly started to evacuate the village. Some 30-40 women and girls were abducted from this village, among them two sisters of a family I had spoken to when I was working on my book. As with many Hindu and Sikh families where women were abducted and almost certainly raped, this family too refused to acknowledge the existence of these sisters, for their history was a history of shame, best forgotten. And here we were, fifty years later, standing on that very same spot, in the slanting, late morning light, being welcomed by people from Thamali. 'Please come,' they insisted to Bir Bahadur Singh, 'please come and bless our house.' Bir Bahadur took a drink of water from the young woman, touched his hand to his brow, and blessed his hostess and her children. 'We don't have time to stop, daughter,' he said to her, 'but I would like to give you something small as a token of my love for you who live in this village now.' With this, he called down to our driver and asked him to bring his bag out of the car. He pulled out two dried coconuts and held them out to the young couple, 'This is a small offering I know, but I would like you to have it. I have lived here, I know that it's not possible to get dried coconuts here. These are for you with my love, with love from your mother, my wife...' and saying this, he embraced these strangers he had met only a few minutes before, touched the bent head of the young woman of the house, and turned to us and said 'come, let us move towards Saintha.'

Twenty minutes later, we rounded a bend in the road and Bir Bahadur suddenly let out a shout of recognition. 'Look, look there,' he said, 'there's my old school. It looks just the same!' We looked. Atop a little ridge stood a small, low-slung building, with a narrow verandah running its length, green painted doors and windows giving on to it. In the yard in front there was a solitary, gnarled tree. It was under this tree, Bir Bahadur told us, that he and his friends had played during their school years, but, he asked, where was everybody? 'It's a holiday today,' we were told by one of the children who had by now attached himself to our little group. 'But many of the students are in the village—you can come and meet them there.'

As often happens in villages when outsiders come, by this time our party had acquired something of a following—a clutch of curioius youngsters offering to help, a few scruffy looking children, a stray dog or two. And as we made our way deeper into the village, this small crowd swelled with the addition of a few other young men. There were no girls of course, nor any women. Within a few minutes we had arrived at a scene of considerable activity: a house was being built. Construction workers—looking, for all the world, exactly like the poor, bedraggled and hungry construction workers one might see in India, their thin wiry bodies blackened by the sun, their only covering a scrap of tattered cloth—were engaged in carrying loads of cement from one place to another, while the owners, two burly, prosperous-looking men stood and watched and supervised. The arrival of our little party caused some excitement. Work stopped. Everyone looked. 'Welcome, welcome,' said the two large men, instantly recognizing us for outsiders, while their welcome was echoed by the little knot of men—friends and neighbours—standing around. 'You're from India sardarji?' they asked, addressing Bir Bahadur, to which he responded, 'Yes, but first I am from here, this is my home.' At this, information was exchanged and we were immediately invited into their home, an older building which stood nearby: 'You can't go away like this— you are our guests, for us you are like God. Come, let us at least give you a cup of tea, a glass of sherbet...' Bir Bahadur thanked them and said that he was anxious to first track his friends down before he settled down to spend any time, and asked their permission to carry on. 'Only,' they said, 'if you promise to stop here on your way back. Are you going to stay the night ? Stay with us.'

We began walking. Some distance in front of us, Basheer spotted three old people shuffling along, weighed down with heavy cloth bags full of provisions. Recognizing two of them as his parents-in-law he rushed up to them and stopped them. We followed. Bir Bahadur introduced himself—Basheer had already given his parents-in-law the background to the story—giving his father's name first. The old man recognized the name although he did not remember Bir Bahadur himself. The woman with them, who'd been standing around silently, suddenly opened her mouth in a wide, toothless grin and poked Bir Bahadur in the chest. 'Are you Biran?' she asked, using the nickname his friends had given him.

'Yes, yes' said Bir Bahadur, somewhat surprised, 'who are you?'

But she wouldn't say. Instead, she looked at him, mischief glinting in her eyes, and asked, 'How is Santo? Is she still alive?' using the nickname for Bir Bahadur's mother Basant Kaur, 'and how is Maano?' referring to his dead sister. I slowly came to realize that the villagers in Saintha did not seem to know about Maan Kaur's death, or the horrible way in which she had died, or if they did, they did not want to make any reference to it directly. Instead, they spoke as if she were still alive.

'Santo is well,' said Bir Bahadur, glossing over the second question, 'she's in Delhi with all her grandchildren, but tell me who are you?'

'I am,' she said with a touch of drama, 'Sadq Khan's wife.'

Bir Bahadur gave a great whoop of joy and, in the next instant, put his arms around her and lifted her off the ground. 'My sister, my sister!' he cried, as tears began to stream down his face. 'Oh my sister, where is my brother? Where is Chachha Sajawal Khan? I heard he had died, is this true? Where is my sister Taj with whom I used to play? I wrote a letter to you all some time ago. Did you get it?....' Questions and more questions. The old woman answered some, avoided others. Later, we learnt that her slight hesitation had been because she no longer had an 'official' status as Sadq Khan's wife. He had taken another, a younger woman, as his wife. But at that time, all we knew was that the first contact had been made. Sadq Khan was alive and he was in the village.

Sadq Khan's father, Sajawal Khan, had been the headman of Saintha village. Although Bir Bahadur's family was the only Sikh family in a village of Muslims they were considered important and given respect because they were both moneylenders and shop-keepers. Sant Raja Singh was respected and trusted by the vil-lagers of Saintha. This is how Bir Bahadur had described it when he spoken to me earlier:

> The Musalmaans used to believe in us, trusted us so much...that for example those who were workers... those who used to serve...if a money order came for someone, no one would go to their homes to deliver it... [The post office] was in Thoa Khalsa and the postman would not reach people's mail to them or get money orders to them. That was why when Musalmaans went away from their homes to work, they would give our address as the place to receive their money orders.... My father used to make entries in his register scrupulously... this belongs to so and so, this belongs to so and so...and then people used to come and

buy their provisions out of this...those people trusted us so much.

In return, however, the Sikhs did not extend the same kind of trust to the Muslims. They practised the customary untouchability of Hindus towards Muslims, refusing to eat anything cooked or touched by them. In Bir Bahadur's words:

> ... if there was any function that we had, then we used to call Musalmaans to our homes, they would eat in our houses, but we would not eat in theirs and this is a bad thing, which I realize now. If they would come to our houses we would have two utensils in one corner of the house, and we would tell them, pick these up and eat in them; they would then wash them and keep them aside and this was such a terrible thing. This was the reason Pakistan was created. If we went to their houses and took part in their weddings and ceremonies, they used to really respect and honour us. They would give us uncooked food, ghee, atta, dal, whatever sabzis they had, chicken and even mutton, all raw. And our dealings with them were so low that I am even ashamed to say it. A guest comes to our house and we say to him, bring those uten sils and wash them, and if my mother or sister have to give him food, they will more or less throw the roti from such a distance, fearing that they may touch the dish and become polluted.... We don't have such low dealings with our lower castes as Hindus and Sikhs did with Musalmaans.

In 1945, when Sant Raja Singh decided he wanted to move his

family and business to Thoa Khalsa because he felt it would be safer, the villagers of Saintha tried hard to dissuade him. We'll keep you safe, they offered, we'll protect you from attacks. But Sant Raja Singh was afraid—he no longer trusted his Muslim friends. There were just too many stories of friends turning into enemies, of old, trusted relationships being betrayed. So he took no heed of their appeals. Once in Thoa, he felt, the family would be safer—should anything happen, the Sikhs could band together and fight. It wasn't like being a lone family in the midst of people who could turn hostile at any moment. The tragedy, of course, was that it was in Thoa Khalsa that the Sikhs became most vulnerable to attacks spread over several days. And the tragedy was further compounded when Sant Raja Singh, Bir Bahadur's father, rejected this offer. I quote from Bir Bahadur's description:

> ... when the trouble started the people came from there
> [Saintha]. You know that Ma Hasina whom I mentioned
> to you, her son, Sajawal Khan, he came to us and said we
> could stay in his house if we wanted to. He came with his
> children. But we were doubtful, and today I feel that
> what he was saying, the expression on his face, his bear
> ing—there was nothing there but sincerity and compas
> sion and we, we misunderstood him. We had all been
> through so much trouble and they came to give us sup
> port, to help us, and we refused.

In many ways, Bir Bahadur's journey to Saintha now, 50 years later, was a journey of penance and reparation. For a half century he had carried within him the guilt of the burden of his family's refusal. He wanted, in some way, to appease this guilt, to lighten the load. 'I just want to go to Saintha,' he had said to me, 'and take the soil of my village and touch it to my head. I need to ask their forgiveness.' What if they will not forgive, I had asked, doubtful. 'Of course they will,' he said, confident, 'after all, once you fight, what is there left but reconciliation, what is there left but forgiveness ?'

Forgiveness, of course, is not so easily asked in something like this. All the time that Bir Bahadur spent in Saintha, neither he, nor anyone else, could bring themselves to refer to the violence that had taken place in Thoa Khalsa. I could not understand, at the time, and I am still unable to do so, whether the villagers of Saintha knew of what had happened to Bir Bahadur's family, to his sister Maan Kaur, whether they knew that so many women had jumped into a well and taken their lives... and yet, I thought, surely they must have known. News, and particularly news of this kind, spreads easily between villages that lie close together, as these did. But whenever anyone asked Bir Bahadur about Maan Kaur—and a few did but others did not, again making me wonder if they knew —he somehow evaded the question. Only once did he say to an old woman who asked: 'she died.' Perhaps this is the way silences build up: Maan Kaur's absence hung in the air in virtually every encounter we had, and yet, apart from the odd question or two, no one explicitly mentioned her.

We made our way further into the village. A small house located at the turn of the narrow strip of road we were following came into view. Bir Bahadur informed us that this used to be a local sweet shop run by someone he knew and soon enough, almost as if on cue, a group of young women, granddaughters and granddaughters-in-law of the man in question, emerged. Yes, they confirmed, there used to be a shop there, but it was closed down after the old man died. The conversation was interrupted by the sudden arrival of a tall, emaciated, scruffy looking old man in a brown shalvar and kurta, and sporting a pencil-thin moustache and short beard. He hesitated for a moment, listening. Then, he fixed Bir Bahadur with a sharp, direct stare and asked: 'Are you Biran ?'

'Yes,' said Bir Bahadur, 'and who are you ?'

'You don't remember me?' he said, 'really, you don't remember me?' I couldn't tell whether he was angry or amused, there was a glint of something in his eyes.

'No, I'm trying,' said Bir Bahadur, 'but I can't. Tell me your name.'

'You bastard,' said the old man, 'you nearly strangled me to death one day ! You jumped on me and almost scratched my throat into ribbons,' he said, gesturing wildly at his throat, and then leaping onto Bir Bahadur and making as if to scratch his throat!

There was one of those moments of perfect stillness. Suddenly, fear was palpable. I realized, in a moment, that no matter that it was more than fifty years after the event, but we had, after all, carried the history of that bitter division with us. I felt a stab of fear at the situation we were in. And then we saw that the old man was chuckling quietly to himself. He had made a joke! This is the story he told us. 'You crazy!' said Bir Bahadur, once he'd been reminded of the story, ' I'll scratch your throat again!' and he leapt on him in mock attack, as the two tangled and laughed and cried at the same time and the old man recounted the story to us.

He and Bir Bahadur had been at school together. It was during that time that Aslam had accepted a dare from his schoolmates to 'pollute' Bir Bahadur's drinking water by putting the earthenware pot in which it was stored to his mouth. Hindus and Muslims did not drink from the same vessel, nor keep their water in the same pot, for fear of pollution—the Hindus, that is, feared the Muslims would pollute their water. It seemed incredible to me that, being the only non-Muslim family in the village, Bir Bahadur's family could still keep to these taboos, but they did. The young Aslam had drunk from Bir Bahadur's pot and had then teased Bir Bahadur about it, at which the incensed young Sikh had attacked his friend and tried to scratch his throat. 'You used to have such long nails then,' shouted Aslam gleefully, 'let me look at your nails now,' grabbing one of Bir Bahadur's hands to examine the length of the nails ! The boys had fought, and had then been gently pried apart by the village elders who had explained to Aslam that he should not have done what he did, that it was important to respect the customs of others. Something, I thought, that we would do well to remember today.

Bir Bahadur had not remembered this particular instance but water and food played a major part in his journey home. 'There are two things I want to do if we make it to Saintha,' he had earlier told me, 'to drink water from the village well and to eat in the home of a Musalmaan.' This was his private penance, his repara-tion, his way of asking forgiveness for the harshness and cruelty of Hindu 'untouchability' and the purity and pollution taboos of the Hindu religion. Now he turned to Aslam and said to him, 'Brother, can you take me to the village well. I want to drink the water from there.' Wordlessly, almost as if he divined what it was that drove Bir Bahadur to make such a request—for between the first instance of playful pollution and today stood a long history of hate and violence—Aslam let us further down the road, to a half-covered well. Two young men from the village were dispatched to find a couple of tumblers, while others lowered the bucket into the well—which looked, at first glance, as if might not be too healthy—and drew up a bucketful of clear, cool, water. Bir Bahadur took the tumbler from the young man who filled it and held it out to him, and touched it to his forehead and drank deeply. He closed his eyes, and seemed to pray as he drank—I could not make out the words, but I thought he was asking forgiveness, not so much for himself but also on behalf of his people—and then be   to ourselves? How could we have allowed ourselves to be divided thus? And then, the spell was broken as two old women, watching us from a balcony above the road, spoke up and asked Bir Bahadur if he was Biran. And he was off again. But not before he had turned to me and offered the remainder of the water to me: 'Here child, you drink also,' he said. After a moment of doubt about how clean or otherwise the water was—after all, the well was open to the sky, even though the water in the bucket looked clear—I decided that there were times when considerations of bacteria and health simply did not matter. I put the glass to my lips and drank.

News of Bir Bahadur's visit had spread in the village and we had suddenly collected quite a large following. We moved on, Bir Bahadur and Aslam in the lead, talking about this field and that crop, and this hillock and that house. We were heading, I guessed, towards Sadq Khan. Finding him, I realized, was not going to be difficult—with the mysterious village grapevine at work, everywhere we went people came out to greet Bir Bahadur, their faces wreathed in smiles of welcome. As if in support of our little expedition, the day remained bright and clear, the heat and humidity miraculously restrained. Bir Bahadur meanwhile did not know whether to laugh or cry—as each new person came up and enfolded him in an embrace, his tears fell with a sort of abandon, drops of moisture glistening on his white beard. 'These are tears of joy, Beta, don't worry,' he reassured me every time I looked at him. 'I am so happy. Did I not tell you we would be welcomed?'

We crossed a small bridge over a nullah, skirted slushy wet mud still recovering from last night's heavy rain, and made our way through some low bushes up a green, grassy slope. Just above us, to the left and right, stood two houses, the one, a makeshift sort of barn and the other an open, airy living space which held three of four old men and women. Between the houses ran a small lane, leading to another house further back. As we wound our way up, people came out of the house to greet Bir Bahadur and began to talk. I suddenly became aware that, for the first time since we had entered Saintha, Bir Bahadur's attention was distracted. He was not listening. Instead, he was looking at the narrow lane which led to the house at the back. Through this, now, came a small, stocky man in a shalvar kurta, a two or three-day stubble on his face, shuffling along with difficulty. As he drew closer, a sort of silence descended on our group and we watched, as he broke away from the clutch of old women and children outside the house and made his painful way down towards us. His face held a smile but his eyes shone with tears. I think both of them knew instantly who the other was but for some moments, it seemed as if we were all caught in a state of suspension. No one could move.

Then, he came within a few steps of Bir Bahadur and said to him, in a whisper, 'Biran, is it really you ? After all these years ?'

And Bir Bahadur, laughing, crying at the same time, thanking God, begging forgiveness, opening his arms wide and saying, 'Sadq, my friend Sadq...the gods be praised... Vahe Guru,' he said, lifting his eyes heavenwards, 'Vahe Guru, my cup is full...' With his arm around Bir Bahadur Sadq Khan turned him gently towards the house and said, 'Come, let me take you to your home.' It was then that I realized that the house at the end of the lane, Sadq Khan's house, was the house that Bir Bahadur had grown up in.

As if on cue, the group of women and children broke into loud chatter. We entered a large courtyard, followed now by our entire entourage and there was a great deal of good natured banter: 'So Biran,' they said to him, 'have you come to take over your house? D'you want your property back? You'll have to tussle with us first you know.' And Bir Bahadur laughing and saying, 'no, no, this is yours not mine, it's yours...' The house lay in a kind of protected hollow: a small field on one side, and a courtyard bordered by two other houses on the other sides, a winding road running behind the house. At one end, young women cooked, their heads covered and faces hidden. We were shown around the house and I thought of the young Maan Kaur, playing with friends here, little knowing the terrible fate that awaited her.

But we were here on work. Suddenly, reminded that we should be paying attention to the radio programme we had come to make, Chihiro thought that this might be a good moment to capture—the two friends meeting after all these years. So she tried to shoo everyone out of the room in which we now sat, a dark, cool room with only one window, much of the space taken up with two beds, a number of trunks, a couple of rexene covered sofas and a table. She turned the fan off: it was making too much noise, she said, and would disturb the recording. Someone immediately turned it back on, and the whirring, grinding noise began. She tried to get the children to go out and the two men to respond to her questions, without success. Eventually, she gave up and decided to just capture the background noises. She'd do her interview with Bir Bahadur later.

Outside, charpais were now laid out in the shade of the old banyan tree and people had begun to congregate there. Years ago, Bir Bahadur had told me the story of Ma Hussaini, a neighbour, who had been like a grandmother to him:

> There was a Musalmaan woman, Dadi, Dadi we used to call her. Her name was Ma Hussaini and I would go and sit on one side of her lap, and her granddaughter would sit on the other. I used to pull her plait and push her away and she would catch hold of my jura, my hair, and push me away. I would say, she is my Dadi, and she would say, she is my Dadi.... It was only after we came here [to India] after Pakistan was created that we realized that this woman we used to call Dadi, she was a Musalmaani. She used to have a garden of fig trees, and she had kept one tree for me and she would not even give the fruit of that tree to the masjid, she had reserved it for me...'

Bir Bahadur's rival in Ma Hussaini's affection, her granddaughter Taj, had been married into a village nearby and had spent some time living in the Middle East with her husband. This Bir Bahadur knew, for while in the Middle East he and Taj had kept in touch. But now, down the slope behind the house came an old woman, hobbling along with the help of a stick—Taj's sister, come to meet her childhood friend. And soon, quite a crowd had collected under the tree. 'Did you ever receive the letters I wrote ?' asked Bir Bahadur of no-one in particular. Yes, he was told, two letters had arrived, one addressed to the village and one to some of the village elders who were now dead, so for a while, they had lain around in the village post box and no one had known what to do with them. Then, they decided to open them and the letters were shared among all those in the village who were there at the time of Partition.

' I wrote you two more,' said Bir Bahadur, 'I was not sure I would be able to come here, so I thought I would send you the letters from Thoa. "

Where are they, he was asked, and he produced them from his pocket. So that everyone could know what was in them, Sadq Khan asked Bir Bahadur to read the letters out. Meanwhile, he and another man with a black scarf tied turban-like on his head, went into the house and came out holding sitars. They strummed gently, as Bir Bahadur read:

> *The First Letter*
> I greet all my brothers and sisters of Saintha village and offer you my salutations. I am Bir Bahadur Singh, son of Sant Raja Singh, who used to run a kirana shop in Saintha. I have come to Pakistan from India to fulfil a long-cher ished dream. All my life I have had but one dream—that is, to be able to come here and meet with all of you, and now I have come to realize this dream. I wanted to come back, to visit again the places where I played as a child, to

meet with all of those people who gave me so much love; I
knew that if I could do this, it would give me real happiness.
I have forgotten the names of so many of you who were
my childhood friends—it has been 54 years since I left
Saintha village—but in my memory I have kept the
names of some of the village elders I remember, and I am
putting them down here: Chacha Mohammad Zaman,
Masi Barkat, Masi Noor Jehan, Chacha Sajawal Khan,
Chacha Sarwar Khan, Chacha Muran who was lame in
one leg, my dear sister Taj, my elder sister Sultana who
was given in marriage to Khodiwala village, Dari who
became my friend at the time of his circumcision. So
many of the children of our elders went to school with
me. Chacha Sajawal Khan's mother, Ma Hussaini, or
Dadi, in whose lap I used to play and under whose loving
care I grew up. I have come to make your acquaintance,
to renew my friendship with the families of our respected
elders. I request you to come from Saintha to meet me
[the letter was written when he did not know whether he
would make it to Saintha]. I will be ever grateful to you
for this. If you can, I will be found at the address given
below. My visa is valid for only 4 days and I will be waiting
for you. I have full faith that you will surely come.
My mother is still alive and it was also her desire that I
come and meet with you once. When you think back on
those old times, you will remember me. I have drunk the
water of the Dhela Dulla stream and the village well, I
still have the taste of Chacha Sarwar's guavas and the fruit
from Khojiwala on my tongue. I remember my teachers,

193

Sargat Ali and Saif Ali from whom I learnt so much. They lived in Sadda village. I studied in Skot school and was the only Sikh there. Those of our elders who are alive, please give my salutations to them, and those who have passed on, I ask you to pay my respects at their graves. For those of you who are alive, I hope you will accept once again the hand of true friendship that I extend to you. I am waiting for you. When you come, please bring me a handful of earth from our beloved Saintha and some water from the Dhulla stream where we played as children. Please also bring some photos and then we can sit and talk here. God be with you and may He protect you.

The Second Letter
My brother Sadq Khan
My beloved Sadq Khan, son of Sajawal Khanji, please accept my greetings. My brother, I am the son of Sant Raja Singh, who used to run a kirana store in Saintha. I have written you letters before this, and have also received replies, but for some time now, I have not written. Please don't think that I have forgotten you and everyone else in Saintha. Every day in my dreams I taste the delicious figs of Dadi's gardens, and I swear to you on God's name that when the dream breaks, and I awaken, I can still taste the sweetness on my tongue. I remember Dadiji, Chacha Sajawal Khan, and everyone from the village —your memories are still fresh in my mind. I remember Arif Bhai, who lost his life while trying to save me from snakebite—perhaps it was that God loved him too much

and took him away. My sister Taj and I used to play in Dadi's lap, we used to fight over who had the right to sit there. I would say Dadi belongs to me and Taj would insist that she belonged to her and Dadi would take us both in her lap and give us abundantly of her love. I have memories of the kharboozas Masi Barkat fed us, the fruit Chacha Sarwar Khan gave us, and so many others... it is with these memories in my heart that I have come from India to see you. I want to greet you and all my friends with whom I studied in Skot school. I have come to Thoa Khalsa and this evening I will return to Islamabad. My visa is only for four days. I beg you to come and meet me. I will do my best to come to Saintha but it may be that I will not be able to come. I am sending you this letter from Thoa Khalsa, please come here to see me.

Your brother
Bir Bahadur Singh (Biran)

The letters read, Bir Bahadur handed them over to Sadq Khan. As his voice faded, the strumming grew louder and soon, a clear, strong voice rose above the noise of conversation, singing songs of loss and joy, welcoming long-lost friends, come from afar. Others joined in, and gradually a silence descended over the gathering, each person thinking his or her private thoughts. The shadows began to lengthen, the sun making its way to its resting place and quietly, tactfully, as the singing continued, we were drawn aside and taken into the house to be fed. As we began to move, we heard a voice say, almost as if in jest: 'our cup is so full, we have even forgotten to eat ! But the guests must be fed, for us this is enough....' Sadq Khan put his sitar down, and followed us into the house where he ate with us, and then we said our goodbyes and set off. A long train of people followed us through the village, some singing, some talking, some just holding Bir Bahadur's hand.

We approached the small road we had taken into the village. Here, the construction work had stopped, but the two men waited for us to make good our promise to spend time with them on the way out. We were taken into the house, a long, shady room, set with sofas in deep red velvet. Small formica-covered tables stood in front of the sofas and on them, three plates of biscuits, and three large bottles of Coca Cola, accompanied by three glasses. We sat, the brothers sitting across from us and sundry other people from the village scattered all about. From behind the chilmans, we could see the shadowy figures of the women of the household watching us—we must have been a strange sight. We had started off thinking this last stop on our journey was merely a formality. It turned out to be quite different. The owners of the house knew all about Bir Bahadur—for it was into their house that the daughter of Arif, the man who had died of snakebite while attempting to save Bir Bahadur from it, was married. For Bir Bahadur, there could have been no better way to end this journey of friendship and reconciliation.

But while one journey had ended the other—to Thoa Khalsa— still remained incomplete. Should we go there or not ? Bir Bahadur's clever sleight-of-hand that morning had initially served to sideline the issue. And now it no longer seemed that urgent. Chihiro had her story—a happy one. In Saintha, they advised us against going—the people of Thoa Khalsa are not good, they said, they do not like strangers. They were being polite of course —they meant Indians, or more precisely, Hindus and Sikhs. [And who could blame them? Every such stranger must have been a reminder of that terrible and violent history of a half century ago.] And I? I wasn't sure. I wondered what kind of reception we would get: in 1947 the population of Thoa had been mostly Sikh. But now, there wasn't a single Sikh left there. Instead, they'd been replaced by Muslims, many of whom must have carried their own tales of violence at the hands of Hindus and Sikhs. Would they even want to see us?

And then, there were other things. I have known Bir Bahadur for more than ten years now. I've interviewed him extensively for my research and we have kept in touch. In all that time, Maan Kaur's story has always remained only at the edges of our conversation. Or perhaps that's not quite true. Bir Bahadur has never hesitated to speak of Maan Kaur, but he has always described her as heroic, a martyr to the cause of the religion, someone who embraced death willingly. I find this difficult to believe. She was sixteen years old. What could she have known or understood about the troubled politics of Partition ? Of the hate and rage that suddenly seemed to have consumed people who had, until then, lived as friends and neighbours ? Could she really have believed that the cause of making a new nation would be better served by her death ? Or indeed by the deaths, the rapes and abductions of countless other women?

For Bir Bahadur these were not the questions that troubled him. Maan Kaur had brought honour to his family, she had done them proud, and he admired her for that. Instead, it was his father towards whom he extended his understanding and compassion.

He said as much to me once. "Imagine," he said, 'imagine, a father who kills his daughter, how much of a victim, how helpless he must be..."

We did not make it to Thoa Khalsa in the end. Not that we did not try. We did, in a half-hearted sort of way. But it turned out that Thoa Khalsa now fell inside Pakistan's atomic ring and was banned to foreigners. We returned to Delhi the next day, our journey done, the radio programme made, a sort of forgiveness asked and given, Maan Kaur's story once again relegated to the realm of silence.

Notes on Contributors

SONIA JABBAR is an independent writer, currently working on a non-fiction book on Kashmir. She was the recipient of the WISCOMP Scholar of Peace Fellowship, 2000.

MINA KUMAR lives in New York.

AMIT CHAUDHURI lives in Calcutta. *Freedom Song,* published in 1998, won the Los Angeles Times Prize for Fiction. His latest novel, *A New World,* was published by Picador. Chaudhuri's criticism, poetry and short stories have been published in several journals including *The London Review of Books, The Times Literary Supplement, The Guardian, The Spectator,* and *The Observer.* He has edited *The Picador Book of Modern Indian Literature,* Picador 2001.

SUKETU MEHTA is a fiction writer and journalist who lives in New York. He is a winner of the Whiting Writers Award, the

O. Henry Prize for his fiction, a New York Foundation for the Arts Fellowship in fiction, and a SAJA award for his journalism. He is currently working on a non-fiction book on Bombay.

AMITAVA KUMAR is the author of *Passport Photos* and a literary columnist on Tehelka.com. He teaches at PennState University.

AVTAR SINGH is Assistant Editor at *Man's World* magazine in Bombay. His first novel, *The Beauty of These Present Things* was published last year.

ANITA ROY is Head of Publishing, Dorling Kindersley, New Delhi.

URVASHI BUTALIA is co-founder of Kali for Women and the author of *The Other Side of Silence,* Viking Penguin 1998.